PEDIGREE OF

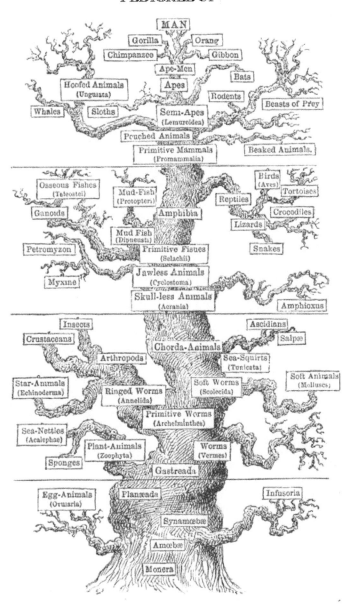

The tree of life as seen by Haeckel in The Evolution of Man (1879)

3

VOLUME ONE

This is **Volume One** of two volumes. Whereas Volume One is devoted, in the main, to the Evolution of the Universe, Galaxies, the Solar System, our Earth, and to the future.Volume Two is more directed to the Evolution of living things.

This is by no means to suggest a clear cut division. In fact whilst it is true to say that the two volumes are essentially mutually exclusive, there is a considerable degree of accordance between the two volumes. One volume supports the other.

First Printing: 2023

979-8-8533-2665-1

Ordering information:
Special discounts are available on quantity purchases
by corporations, associations, educators, and others.

U.S. trade bookstores and wholesalers:
Please contact author at:
e-mail: jamesfrayne2014@hotmail.com
or direct to www.jamesfrayne.co.uk

All tables, charts, maps and animal line drawings are
available as prints in A4 at competitive prices.
For details, contact the author at the e-mail address
detailed below.

Front Cover   _Section of Charles R. Knight's 1920_
reconstruction: Magdalenian painters
at Font-de-Gaume, France.PD

_This classic Knight mural from the American Museum of
Natural History depicts a Cro-Magnon artist painting
mammoths near the entrance of Font-de-Gaume, France._

For more details please visit author's website at:
http://jamesfrayne.co.uk

By the same author:

Tall Grows the Grass (African Historical Novel)
First Son of Khui (Egyptian Historical Novel)

'SHE' (Anthology of Women in Mathematic and Science)

Easy as you Go! A Mathematical Companion
(Volume 1: A – L)
Easy as you Go! A Mathematical Companion
(Volume 2: M- Z)
A-Star Question Bank
(Mathematics with or without solutions)
Mathematics & Statistics for Biology, Psychology & Chemistry

Mathematics by Stages (Angles to Vectors)
Mathematics by Stages (Circles and Curves)
Mathematics by Stages (Advanced Topics)

Hell Bank Notes (A Pictorial Catalogue)
Romancing the Wood
(History behind the American Wooden Nickel)
The Indian Hundi
(Favourite negotiable instrument in days gone by)
Hidden Stories behind Paper Money around the World

Selected Biology Advance Level Topics (Volume 1: A – J)
Selected Biology Advance Level Topics (Volume 2: K – Z)

Greenhouse Effect
Mechanics (The Basics)

Jenny Two-tails and her Friends (Book for Young Children)

Applications of Genetics
Atoms and Fundamental Particles

Contents (Volume One)

Contents (Volume Two)

Raphus cucullatus
*The **dodo** is an extinct flightless bird that was endemic to the island of Mauritius. The closest living relative of the dodo is the Nicobar pigeon.*

Tick off all those questions that you can answer with confidence before you read any further.

Come back when you have read <u>the two volumes</u> of 'EVOLUTION (Singularity to the Future)' and tick off all the questions for a second time.

☐ Are there such things as 'friendly viruses'?

☐ Are viruses alive?

☐ Did early Trilobites really have crystals for eyes?

☐ Did the Opabinia really have five eyes?

☐ Do humans have tails?

☐ How can 'flicker fusion rate' protect the Housefly?

☐ How fast does Earth travel through space?

☐ How is Teleology possibly significant to Evolution theory?

☐ How many eyes do Scallops have?

☐ How many teeth do snails have?

☐ How were prehistoric animals assisted in their breathing?

☐ Is the Planaria truly immortal?

☐ What animal had one single orifice to serve for both ingesting and excretion?

☐ What animal had properties far ahead of the evolutionary process?

☐ What animal has over two hundred separate eyes?

☐ What animal possessed tooth whorls?

☐ What are considered to be the closest living relatives to animals?

☐ What are the objections to Darwinian Theory of Natural Selection?

☐ What are the properties of all the greenhouse gases?

☐ What are the two major elements in the Sun?

☐ What are tomia?

- What are Ur and Vaalbara?
- What are vibrissae?
- What damage will the collision of Milky Way with the Andromeda galaxy cause?
- What does the Drake Equation imply?
- What does the Malthusian Theory of Population predict?
- What does Titus-Bode Law state?
- What happened for the Miller-Urey Experiment to be so significant?
- What important findings were made on the Galapagos Islands?
- What important step was made by Leonardo da Vinci?
- What is a Main Sequence star?
- What is a nictitating membrane?
- What is anoxic water?
- What is Burgess Shale?
- What is Cosmic Microwave Expansion?
- What is de Sitter Expansion?
- What is Grand Unified Theory and what are the four forces in nature?
- What is Hachimoji DNA?
- What is Hardy-Weinberg's contribution to Microevolution?
- What is methane clathrate?
- What is Methanosarcina?
- What is so highly significant about the Charnia?
- What is so important about the Precambrian Period?
- What is so special about a Tardigrade?
- What is so special about Iridium?
- What is so special about the Gaia-Enceladus galaxy?
- What species is believed to be the earliest example of a primate?

- [ ] What is the connection of Evolution to Global Warming and the Greenhouse Effect?
- [ ] What is the Escape Velocity from Earth?
- [ ] What is the essential idea behind the 'Out of Africa' Hypothesis?
- [ ] What is the Genetic Code?
- [ ] What is the Geologic Time Scale?
- [ ] What is the Kardashev Scale?
- [ ] What is the Multiregional Hypothesis?
- [ ] What is theorized to have happened to the planetoid called Theia?
- [ ] What makes Murchison meteorite special?
- [ ] What Prosimians were believed to be ancestral to Hominids?
- [ ] What significant event caused the Dinosaurs to become extinct?
- [ ] What term did Herbert Spencer introduce in his quest for an understanding of the origin and destiny of all living things?
- [ ] What were the first examples of prehistoric art?
- [ ] What were the functions of the 24 eyes of a Box Jellyfish?
- [ ] What were the key events in the Geological Timeline?
- [ ] What will happen to Homo sapiens in future years?
- [ ] What will happen to the Earth, the Solar System and the Milky Way in future years?
- [ ] When did Archbishop Usher calculate that God created man?
- [ ] When did Multi-cellular life first appear?
- [ ] When did the 'Great Dying' occur?
- [ ] When did the brain of Homo sapiens cease to grow?
- [ ] When did the Chicxulub Impact Event occur?
- [ ] When did the first warm-blooded animals appear?
- [ ] When was the Great Oxidation Event?
- [ ] When was the Solar System formed?
- [ ] When will oxygen run out?

- Where can Golden Jellyfish be found?
- Where did the water in all the oceans come from?
- Where do viruses come from?
- Who advanced the idea that the physical world's remote history can be inferred from evidence in present-day rocks?
- Who championed the idea of continuity and gradual change in early civilization?
- Who was Lucy?
- Who were the Cro Magnon?
- Why is the Sixth Extinction Event so significant to life on Earth?

Cro Magnon
Wounded deer from Peña de Candamo, Spain

Preface

*'Evolution is the process of continuous developments over time and by which process such inherent changes are evidenced by positive traits leading to further enhancements and a combination of interrelated phenomena, or to **negative incompatible traits ending with extinction**.'*

Evolution in all its various forms has come a long way from the split second after the Big Bang until the present day.

In 'Metaphysics' Aristotle states 'the more you know, the more you know you don't know' and it is this principle that has goaded 'civilization' to greater ends. The knowledge that *Homo sapiens* has gained about the past 13.77 billion years of the Universe's existence has been unparalleled.

Yet there are probably more things we do not know now about life, our purpose in living, our destiny. Though not since the last Mass Extinction some 66 million years ago has life been in so much danger of extinction than it is right now.

Ever since the beginning of the Industrial Revolution around the 1750s technology has developed exponentially. But the knowledge that we have gained has come at a dreadful price. Industrialization and an incomplete appreciation of the effects it has had, and continues to have, on life and evolution in general cannot be ignored.

The current geological age, the so-called **Anthropocene Age**, is viewed somewhat magnanimously as the period during which human activity has been the dominant influence on climate and the environment. Rather more than this though, and one that has far more implications; it is as if the lights of present-day life are sadly and unquestionably going out one-by-one.

We have now begun to suffer from the effects of wanton pollution of our planet and lack of control in carbon emissions. The consequences of this are manifold: degradation of the environment, increased risk to the health of both fauna and flora (and that includes humans), ozone layer depletion, land infertility, global warming … the list goes on…!

But all these consequences have a serious bearing on Evolution; they are all the '**negative incompatible traits which could well end in extinction**'.

There is ample evidence of the consequences, not least of all in widespread floods and forest fires that are now blighting large areas of the world. What is perhaps not so evident is the alarming loss of species, many of which are fundamental to the well-being of *H. sapiens* in one way or another.

It is sincerely hoped that this book will be instrumental in bringing home an awareness of the many paths, the twists and turns, the trials and tribulations that nature has gone through in order for *H. sapiens* to become the species it has become today.

But just as importantly, it is hoped that this book will leave the reader more appreciative of the Universe in which everybody and everything plays such a momentous part, and to the ever-changing nature of life which could perhaps hold such a wonderful fulfilling future for many billions of years to come were the present threats to world survival be addressed in earnest before it is too late.

James F Frayne
2023

PS The discerning reader will note repetitions in some areas – this is deliberate and is intended to help give a fuller picture of the specific topic then being addressed.

Index of Illustrations
(Volume One)

Helicoprion (290 – 270 Mya)
Helicoprion had a tight, curled-up coil of triangular teeth, a bit like a Swiss roll, but considerably deadlier. As far as palaeontologists can tell, this bizarre structure was attached to the bottom part of Helicoprion's jaw.

Animals & Fossils

Choanoflagellate

The Choanoflagellates are a group of free-living unicellular and colonial flagellate eukaryotes considered to be the closest living relatives of the animals.

World Maps

Information Sheets

Nicolaus Copernicus
Copernicus was a Renaissance   polymath, active as a mathematician, astronomer, and Catholic canon, who formulated a model of the universe that placed the Sun rather than Earth at its centre.

Evolution of the Universe

The universe that we know has been around for 13.772 billion years according to current estimates. Yet nothing is known of the nature of things before the Big Bang and which set off the sequence of events that have brought us to the present day.

We can surmise and construct models, but that is as far as we can go. Leastwise at the moment!

We are though reasonably sure of the events as and when they happened following the Big Bang.

It is these events which are detailed in the ensuing pages.

Before the Big Bang

To best place the sequences of events after the Big Bang it is useful to look at one of the prevailing theories concerning what possibly happened before the Big Bang.

Theorists begin with two flat, homogenous, and parallel three-branes which represent the lowest energy state. Originally, they start empty, cold universes, but gravity gradually pulls them together. They eventually collide, and the vast kinetic energy of the collision is converted into the matter and radiation making up our universe.

The force of the collision pushes the two universes apart. As these two membranes separate from each other, they cool rapidly giving us the universe we see today.

The cooling and expansion continue for trillions of years, until the universes approach absolute zero in temperature and the density is only one electron per quadrillion cubic light-years of space. In effect, the universe becomes empty and inert.

But gravity continues to attract the two membranes, until trillions of years later, they collide once again, and the cycle repeats all over again.

Perhaps the greatest joint contribution of the COBE and WMAP satellites and the HUBBLE, SDSS and JWSD telescopes is that it gives scientists confidence that they are headed toward a '**Standard Model**' of cosmology. (*refer to Chapter 03 - Mapping the Universe*).

Although huge gaps still exist, astrophysicists are beginning to see outlines of a 'standard theory' emerging from the data. According to the picture we are putting together now, the evolution of the universe proceeded in distinct stages as it cooled.

The transition from these stages represents the breaking of symmetry and the splitting off of a force of nature.

Here are the major phases and milestones as we know and begin to understand them today:

Before 10^{-43} seconds – Planck Epoch (10^{32} K)

It is quite probable that the universe may have existed in a perfect phase of 'nothingness', or empty higher dimensional space.

It began with a cataclysm that generated space and time, as well as all the matter and energy the universe holds today and will ever hold. For an incomprehensibly small fraction of a second, the universe was an infinitely dense, hot fireball.

Admittedly, however, practically nothing is certain about the **Planck epoch** and a good deal is, for the time being, pure conjecture. At **Planck energy**, the gravitational force was as strong as the other three quantum forces (*see later*) and, as a consequence, the four forces of the universe were all probably unified into a single 'super-force'.

The general theory describes a peculiar form of energy that can suddenly push out the fabric of space, and the mysterious symmetry that unifies all the forces, leaving the equations the same, is most likely 'super-symmetry'.

For reasons yet unknown, the unification of all the four forces was broken and a tiny bubble formed, our embryonic universe, perhaps as the result of a random quantum fluctuation. This bubble was the size of the **'Planck length'** which is 10^{-33} centimetres.

10^{-36} seconds – Grand Unified Theory Epoch (GUT) (10^{29} K)

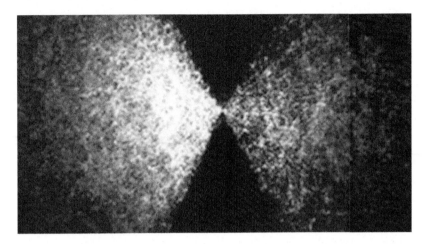

Symmetry breaking occurred, creating a rapidly expanding bubble. As the bubble inflated, the four fundamental forces rapidly split off from each other.

Gravity was the first force to be split off from the other three, releasing a shock wave throughout the then universe. The original symmetry of the super-force was broken down to a smaller symmetry, but the remaining weak, electromagnetic and strong forces were still unified by this GUT symmetry.

The universe inflated by an enormous factor, perhaps 10^{50}. During this phase, for reasons that are not yet understood, this causes space to expand astronomically faster than the speed of light.

10^{-32} to 10^{-33} seconds – Inflationary Epoch (10^{28} K – 10^{22} K)

A runaway process called '**Inflation**' causes a vast expansion of space filled with this energy. The inflationary epoch is stopped only when this energy is transformed into matter and energy as we know it.

As the temperature drops dramatically the strong force splits off from the other two forces. The inflationary epoch ends, allowing the Universe to coast in a standard '**Friedmann expansion**'.

At this stage, the Universe consisted of a hot plasma 'soup' of free quarks, gluons, and leptons, the free quarks condensing into the protons and neutrons of today.

Our Universe, though, is still quite small being only the size of the present solar system. Matter and antimatter are annihilated, but the tiny excess of matter over antimatter (one part per billion) is left behind as the matter we see around us today.

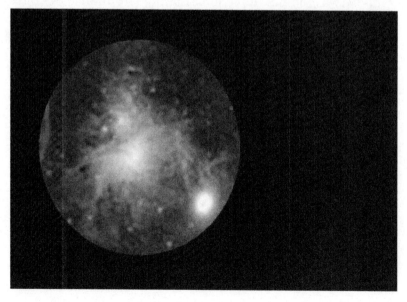

10^{-32} seconds to 10 seconds
The Universe takes shape
(10^{15} K – 10^9 K)

After inflation, **one millionth of a second after the Big Bang**, the Universe continues to expand but not nearly so quickly. As it expands, it becomes less dense and cools.

The most basic forces in nature become distinct: first gravity, then the strong force, which holds nuclei of atoms together, followed by the weak and electromagnetic forces.

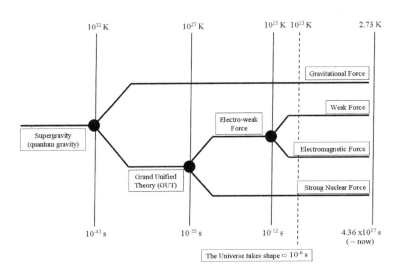

By the first second, the Universe is now made up of **fundamental particles** and **energy**: quarks, electrons, photons, neutrinos and less familiar types.

25

3 minutes from Big Bang
Formation of Basic Elements
(10^9 K – 10^7 K)

Temperatures drop sufficiently for nuclei to form without being ripped apart from the intense heat.

Protons and neutrons come together to form the nuclei of simple elements: hydrogen, helium and lithium. It will take another 370,000 years for electrons to be captured into orbits around these nuclei to form stable atoms.

Hydrogen fuses into helium (creating the current 75% hydrogen / 25% helium ratio found today).

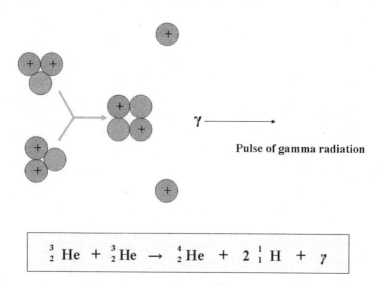

Pulse of gamma radiation

$$^3_2 He + {}^3_2 He \rightarrow {}^4_2 He + 2\,{}^1_1 H + \gamma$$

Trace amounts of lithium are formed, but the fusion of higher elements stops because nuclei with five particles are too unstable.

The Universe is now opaque, with light being scattered by free electrons.

10,000 years from Big Bang
The Radiation Era
($>10^4$ K)

The first major era in the history of the Universe is one in which most of the energy is in the form of radiation, different wavelengths of light, X rays, radio waves and ultra-violet rays.

This energy is the remnant of the primordial fireball, and as the Universe expands, the waves of radiation are stretched and diluted until today they make up the faint glow of microwaves which bathe the entire Universe.

300,000 years from Big Bang
Atoms are born
The beginning of Matter Domination
(4,000 K)

At this moment, the energy in matter and the energy in radiation are equal. But as the relentless expansion continues, the waves of light are stretched to lower and lower energy, while the matter travels onward largely unaffected.

At about this time, neutral atoms are formed as electrons link up with hydrogen and helium nuclei. The **microwave background radiation** hails from this moment, and thus gives us a direct picture of how matter was distributed at this early time.

The temperature drops to 4,000 Kelvin. Atoms form as electrons settle around nuclei without being ripped apart by the heat. Photons can now travel freely without being absorbed.

This is the radiation measured by COBE and WMAP.

The Universe, once opaque and filled with plasma, now becomes transparent.

The sky, instead of being white, becomes black.

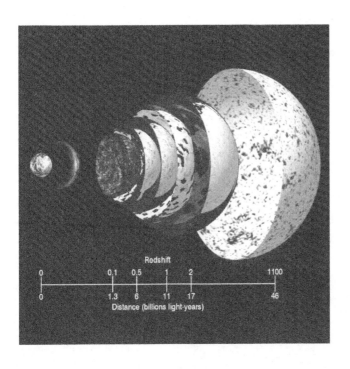

Redshift

| 0 | 0.1 | 0.5 | 1 | 2 | 1100 |

| 0 | 1.3 | 6 | 11 | 17 | 46 |

Distance (billions light-years)

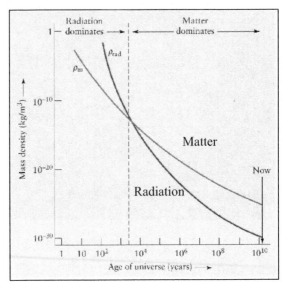

*The early radiation dominated universe
became today's matter dominated universe.*

29

300 million years from Big Bang
Birth of Stars and Galaxies
(60K)

Gravity amplifies slight irregularities in the density of the primordial gas. Even as the Universe continues to expand rapidly, pockets of gas become more and more dense.

Stars ignite within these pockets, and groups of stars become the earliest galaxies. This point is still perhaps 12 to 15 billion years before the present.

1 billion years from Big Bang
Stars condense
(18K)

Quasars, galaxies, and galactic clusters begin to condense, largely as a by-product of tiny quantum ripples in the original fireball. Stars begin to 'cook' the light elements, like carbon, oxygen, and nitrogen. Exploding stars spewed elements beyond iron into the heavens.

This is the farthest era that can be probed by the Hubble space telescope. The James Webb Space Telescope (*see later*), however, has now become the largest, most powerful space telescope ever built. It has already allowed scientists to look at what our universe was like about 200 million years after the **Big Bang**.

6.5 billion years from Big Bang
De Sitter expansion
(2.67 K)

What is referred to as the 'Friedmann expansion' gradually ends, and the Universe begins to accelerate and enter an accelerating phase, called the 'De Sitter expansion', driven by a mysterious anti-gravity force that is still not understood.

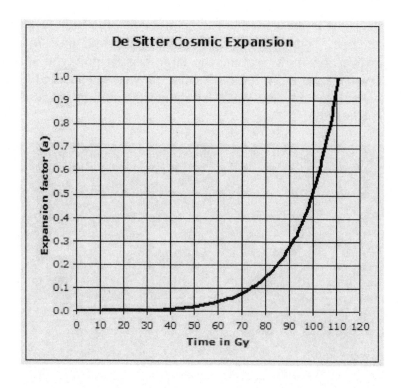

8 – 9 Billion years from Big Bang
4.6 Billion years ago
Birth of the Sun
(>1.5 x 10^6 K)

The Sun forms within a cloud of gas in a spiral arm of the **Milky Way Galaxy**. A vast disk of gas and debris that swirls around this new star which gives birth to planets, moons, and asteroids. Earth is the third planet out.

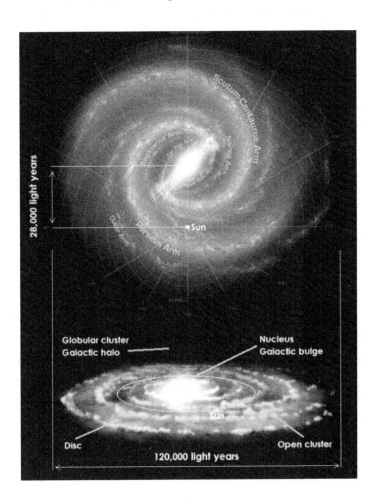

10 Billion years from Big Bang
3.7 Billion years ago
Earliest Life on Earth
(> 200 K)

The Earth has cooled and an atmosphere develops. Microscopic living cells, but not plants nor animals, begin to evolve and flourish in Earth's many volcanic environments.

At this time, the **water condenses into rain** which fills the basins that are now our oceans. Most scientists agree that the atmosphere and the oceans accumulated gradually over millions and millions of years with the continual 'degassing' of the Earth's interior. According to this theory, the ocean formed from the escape of water vapour and other gases from the molten rocks of the Earth to the atmosphere surrounding the cooling planet.

750 Mya – Multi-cellular Life Appears

Even the most primitive of life forms would be dependent on the presence of the essential elements being present. These life forms were mostly flatworms, jelly fish and algae.

By 540 million years before the present, large numbers of creatures with hard shells suddenly appeared.

Periodic Table of Elements in the Human Body

Key:
- Essential elements (incl. Trace)
- Non-essential elements

H																	He
Li	Be											B	C	N	O	F	
Na	Mg											Al	Si	P	S	Cl	
K	Ca	Sc	Ti	V	Cr	Mn	Fe	Co	Ni	Cu	Zn	Ga	Ge	As	Se	Br	
Rb	Sr	Y	Zr	Nb	Mo					Ag	Cd	In	Sn	Sb	Te	I	
Cs	Ba		Ta	W						Au	Hg	Tl	Pb	Bi			
	Ra																

	La	Ce				Sm											
		Th		U													

The **Cambrian explosion** or Cambrian radiation was an event approximately 540 million years ago at this time known as the Cambrian period when practically all major animal phyla started appearing in the fossil record.

It lasted for about 53.4 million years and resulted in the divergence of most modern metazoan phyla.

Element	Symbol	Percentage in Body
Oxygen	O	65.0
Carbon	C	18.5
Hydrogen	H	9.5
Nitrogen	N	3.2
Calcium	Ca	1.5
Phosphorus	P	1.0
Potassium	K	0.4
Sulphur	S	0.3
Sodium	Na	0.2
Chlorine	Cl	0.2
Magnesium	Mg	0.1
Trace elements include boron (B), chromium (Cr), cobalt (Co), copper (Cu), fluorine (F), iodine (I), iron (Fe), manganese (Mn), molybdenum (Mo), selenium (Se), silicon (Si), tin (Sn), vanadium (V), and zinc (Zn).		less than 1.0

Elements present in the Human Body

Major Elements of the Human Body

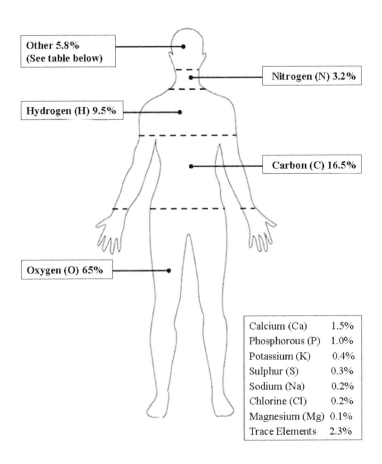

Other 5.8%
(See table below)

Nitrogen (N) 3.2%

Hydrogen (H) 9.5%

Carbon (C) 16.5%

Oxygen (O) 65%

Calcium (Ca)	1.5%
Phosphorous (P)	1.0%
Potassium (K)	0.4%
Sulphur (S)	0.3%
Sodium (Na)	0.2%
Chlorine (Cl)	0.2%
Magnesium (Mg)	0.1%
Trace Elements	2.3%

290 Mya – First Bilateral Mammals Appear

The first mammals were descended from mammal-like reptiles, called **pelycosaurs** that lived on Earth about 290 Mya.

Consequently, the mammals evolved from a class of reptiles that evolved mammalian traits, such as a segmented jaw and a series of bones that make up the inner ear.

The first warm-blooded animals - being warm-blooded is a basic feature of all mammals - were probably the *cynodonts*, which first evolved about 260 million years ago.

The *cynodonts* are a clade of *therapsids* that first appeared in the Late Permian (approximately 260 Mya), and extensively diversified after the Permian–Triassic extinction event.

Cynodonts had a wide variety of lifestyles, including carnivory and herbivory. Mammals (including humans) are *cynodonts*, as are their extinct ancestors and close relatives, having evolved from advanced *probainognathian** *cynodonts* during the Late Triassic. All other cynodont lines went extinct, with the last known non-mammalian *cynodont* group, the *tritylodontidae* having its last records in the Early Cretaceous.

The *cynodonts* probably had some form of warm-blooded metabolism. Being endothermic they may have needed it for thermoregulation, but fossil evidence of their fur (or lack thereof) has been elusive.

Modern mammals have *Harderian glands* secreting lipids to coat their fur, but the tell-tale imprint of this structure is only found from the mammalian order *Morganucodonta* and onwards.

Megazostrodon is an extinct genus belonging to the order *Morganucodonta.* It is approximately 200 million years old.

Two species are known: *M. rudnerae* from the Early Jurassic of Lesotho and South Africa, and *M. chenali* from the Late Triassic of France.

* The probainognathian are members of one of the two major clades of the infraorder Eucynodontia, the other being Cynognathia. The earliest forms were carnivorous and insectivorous, though some groups eventually also evolved herbivorous diets.

66 Mya - Dinosaurs Become Extinct

An asteroid or comet slams into the northern part of the Yucatan Peninsula in Mexico. This world-wide cataclysm brings to an end the long age of the dinosaurs, and allows mammals to diversify and expand their ranges.

200,000 years ago – *Homo sapiens* Evolves

Our earliest ancestor evolves in Africa and possible other areas of the world from a line of creatures that descended from apes.

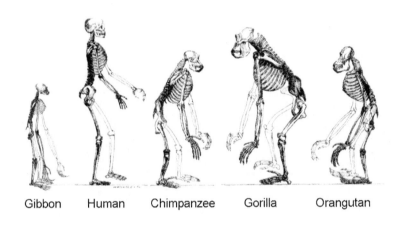

Gibbon   Human   Chimpanzee   Gorilla   Orangutan

13.772 Billion years from the Big Bang

The Present Day

The temperature has dropped to 2.73 degrees Kelvin.

We see the present universe of galaxies, stars, and planets.

The universe is continuing to accelerate in a runaway mode.

Drake Equation

The Drake equation is a probabilistic argument used to estimate the number of active, communicative extraterrestrial civilizations in the Milky Way galaxy.

The equation was formulated in 1961 by Frank Drake, not for purposes of quantifying the number of civilizations, but as a way to stimulate scientific dialogue at the first scientific meeting on the search for extraterrestrial intelligence (SETI).

$$N = R^* \cdot f_p \cdot n_e \cdot f_l \cdot f_i \cdot f_c \cdot L$$

The equation summarizes the main concepts which scientists must contemplate when considering the question of other radio-communicative life.

It is more properly thought of as an approximation than as a serious attempt to determine a precise number. Criticism related to the Drake equation focuses not on the equation itself, but on the fact that the estimated values for several of its factors are highly conjectural, the combined multiplicative effect being that the uncertainty associated with any derived value is so large that the equation cannot be used to draw firm conclusions.

What is referred to as the Fermi Paradox exists in that the Drake equation statistically indicates life should be abundant and yet physical evidence says otherwise. In other words "*where is everybody?*"

Elements of the Drake Equation

N   The number of civilizations in our galaxy with which communication might be possible;

$R*$ The average rate of star formation per year in our galaxy

f_p The fraction of those stars that have planets

n_e The average number of planets that can potentially support life per star that has planets

f_ℓ The fraction of the above that actually go on to develop life at some point

f_i The fraction of the above that actually go on to develop intelligent life

f_c The fraction of civilizations that develop a technology that releases detectable signs of their existence into space

L   The length of time such civilizations release detectable signals into space.

44

Cosmic Microwave Background

The **cosmic microwave background** in Big Bang cosmology is electromagnetic radiation which is a remnant from an early stage of the Universe, also known as '**relic radiation**'.

It is an important source of data on the early Universe because it is the oldest electromagnetic radiation from when the Universe was just 380,000 years old.

One of the profound observations of the 20th century is that the Universe is expanding. This expansion implies the universe was smaller, denser and hotter in the distant past. When the visible universe was half its present size, the density of matter was eight times higher and the cosmic microwave background was twice as hot. When the visible universe was one hundredth of its present size, the cosmic microwave background was a hundred times hotter (273.15 degrees above absolute zero or zero degrees Celsius).

In addition to this cosmic microwave background radiation, the early universe was filled with hot hydrogen gas with a density of about 1000 atoms per cubic centimetre. When the visible universe was only one hundred millionth its present size, its temperature was 273.15 million degrees above absolute zero and the density of matter was comparable to the density of air at the Earth's surface. At these high temperatures, the hydrogen was completely ionized into free protons and electrons.

Since the universe was so very hot through most of its early history, there were no atoms in the early universe, only free electrons and nuclei. (Nuclei are made of neutrons and protons). The cosmic microwave background photons easily scatter off from electrons. Thus, photons wandered through the early universe, just as optical light wanders through a dense fog. This process of multiple scattering produces what is called a 'thermal' or 'blackbody' spectrum of photons. According to the Big Bang theory, the frequency spectrum of the CMB should have this blackbody form. This was indeed measured with tremendous accuracy by the FIRAS experiment by NASA's COBE satellite.

ref: NASA

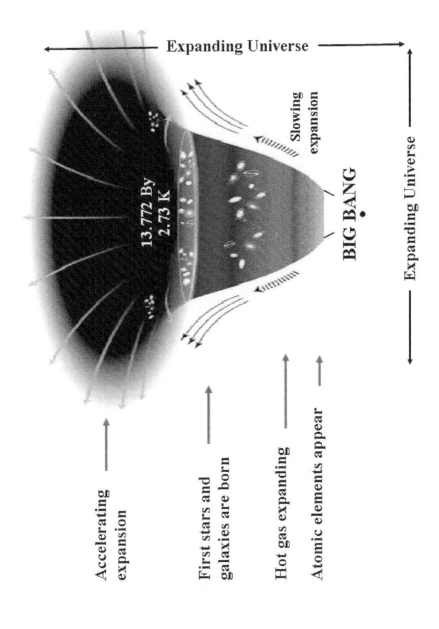

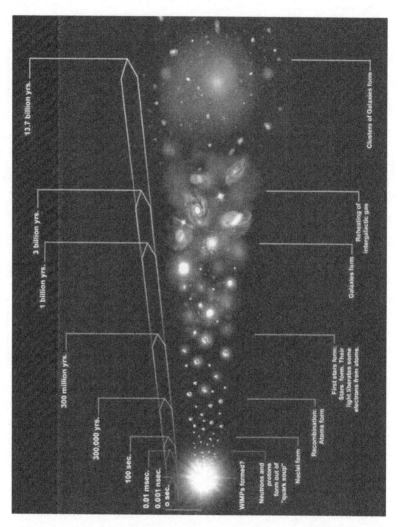

A visual history of the expanding Universe includes the hot, dense state known as the Big Bang and the growth and formation of structure subsequently. The full suite of data, including the observations of the light elements and the Cosmic Microwave Background, leaves only the Big Bang as a valid explanation for all we see.
(NASA / CXC / M. WEISS)

Mapping the Universe

The earliest Greek and Indian models of the universe were geocentric, placing Earth at the centre. More precise astronomical observations led Copernicus to develop the heliocentric model with the Sun at the centre of the Solar System.

Yet further observations led to the realization that the Sun is one of hundreds of billions of stars in the Milky Way, which is one of a few hundred billion galaxies in the universe.

Many of the stars in a galaxy have planets.

Discoveries in the early 20th century have suggested that the universe had a beginning and that space has been expanding since then at an increasing rate.

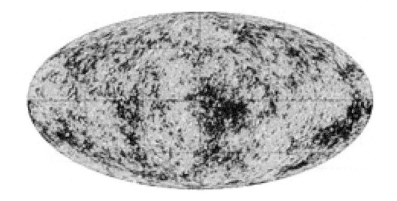

COBE
(Cosmic Background Explorer)

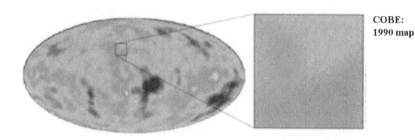

COBE:
1990 map

The **cosmic microwave background (CMB, CMBR)** in Big Bang cosmology is electromagnetic radiation which is a remnant from an early stage of the universe, also known as 'relic radiation'. The CMB is faint cosmic background radiation filling all space. It is an important source of data on the early universe because it is the oldest electromagnetic radiation in the universe, dating to the epoch of recombination. With a traditional optical telescope, the space between stars and galaxies (the background) is completely dark. However, a sufficiently sensitive radio telescope shows a faint background noise, or glow, almost isotropic, that is not associated with any star, galaxy, or other object. This glow is strongest in the microwave region of the radio spectrum. The accidental discovery of the CMB in 1965 by American radio astronomers Arno Penzias and Robert Wilson was the culmination of work initiated in the 1940s, and earned the discoverers the 1978 Nobel Prize in Physics.

CMB is landmark evidence of the Big Bang origin of the universe. When the universe was young, before the formation of stars and planets, it was denser, much hotter, and filled with an opaque fog of hydrogen plasma.

As the universe expanded, both the plasma and the radiation filling it grew cooler. When the temperature had dropped enough, protons and electrons combined to form neutral hydrogen atoms. Unlike the plasma, these newly conceived atoms could not scatter the thermal radiation by Thomson scattering, and so the universe became transparent. Cosmologists refer to the time period when neutral atoms first formed as the *recombination epoch*, and the event shortly afterwards when photons started to travel freely through space is referred to as photon decoupling. The photons that existed at the time of photon decoupling have been propagating ever since, though growing fainter and less energetic, since the

expansion of space causes their wavelength to increase over time (and wavelength is inversely proportional to energy according to Planck's relation). This is the source of the alternative term *relic radiation*. The *surface of last scattering* refers to the set of points in space at the right distance from us so that we are now receiving photons originally emitted from those points at the time of photon decoupling.

WMAC
(Wilkinson Microwave Anisotropy Probe)

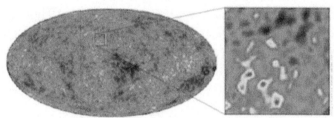

WMAP:
2013 map
(5 times more
sensitive than
COBE)

The Wilkinson Microwave Anisotropy Probe (WMAP), originally known as the Microwave Anisotropy Probe (MAP), is an inactive un-crewed spacecraft operating from 2001 to 2010 which measured temperature differences across the sky in the cosmic microwave background (CMB) – the radiant heat remaining from the Big Bang. Headed by Professor Charles L. Bennett of Johns Hopkins University, the mission was developed in a joint partnership between the NASA Goddard Space Flight Centre and Princeton University.

The WMAP spacecraft was launched on 30th June, 2001 from Florida. The WMAP mission succeeded the COBE space mission and was the second medium-class (MIDEX) spacecraft in the NASA Explorers program. In 2003, MAP was renamed WMAP in honour of cosmologist David Todd Wilkinson (1935–2002), who had been a member of the mission's science team.

After nine years of operations, WMAP was switched off in 2010, following the launch of the more advanced Planck spacecraft by European Space Agency in 2009. WMAP's measurements played a key role in establishing the current Standard Model of Cosmology: the Lambda-CDM model.

The WMAP data are very well fit by a universe that is dominated by dark energy in the form of a cosmological constant.

Other cosmological data are also consistent, and together tightly constrain the Model. In the Lambda-CDM model of the universe, the age of the universe is 13.772 ±0.059 billion years. The WMAP mission's determination of the age of the universe is to better than 1% precision. The current expansion rate of the universe is (Hubble constant) 69.32 ±0.80 km^s Mpc. The content of the universe currently consists of 4.628% ±0.093% ordinary baryonic matter; 24.02% +0.88% −0.87% cold dark matter (CDM) that neither emits nor absorbs light; and 71.35% +0.95% −0.96% of dark energy in the form of a cosmological constant that accelerates the expansion of the universe.

PLANCK
(Named after Max Planck, a notable
German theoretical physicist)

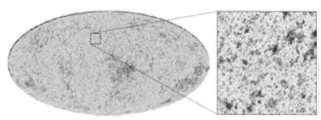

PLANCK:
2013 map
(15 times more
sensitive than
COBE)

Planck was a space observatory operated by the European Space Agency (ESA) from 2009 to 2013, which mapped the anisotropies of the cosmic microwave background (CMB) at microwave and infrared frequencies, with high sensitivity and small angular resolution. The mission substantially improved upon observations made by the NASA Wilkinson Microwave Anisotropy Probe (WMAP). *Planck* provided a major source of information relevant to several cosmological and astrophysical issues, such as testing theories of the early Universe and the origin of cosmic structure.

Since the end of its mission, *Planck* has defined the most precise measurements of several key cosmological parameters, including the average density of ordinary matter and dark matter in the Universe and the age of the universe.

The project was started around 1996 and was initially called **COBRAS/SAMBA**: the Cosmic Background Radiation Anisotropy Satellite/Satellite for Measurement of Background Anisotropies. It was later renamed in honour of the German physicist Max Planck (1858–1947), who derived the formula for black-body radiation.

The Planck space observatory (2009 – 2013)

SDSS
(Sloan Digital Sky Survey)

The **Sloan Digital Sky Survey** is a major survey using a dedicated 2.5m wide-angle optical telescope at Apache Point Observatory in New Mexico, United States.

In July 2020, after a 20 year long survey, astrophysicists published the largest, most detailed 3D map of the universe so far, filled a gap of 11 billion years in its expansion history, and provided data which supports the theory of a flat geometry of the universe and confirms that different regions seem to be expanding at different speeds.

Every night the telescope produces about 200 gigabytes of data.

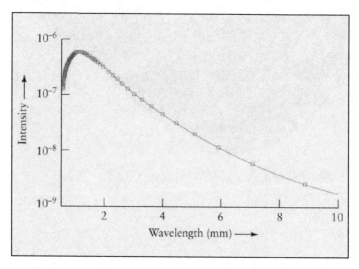

*The spectrum of the Cosmic Microwave Background Radiation reveals a present-day temperature of **2.725 +/- 0.002 degrees Kelvin.***

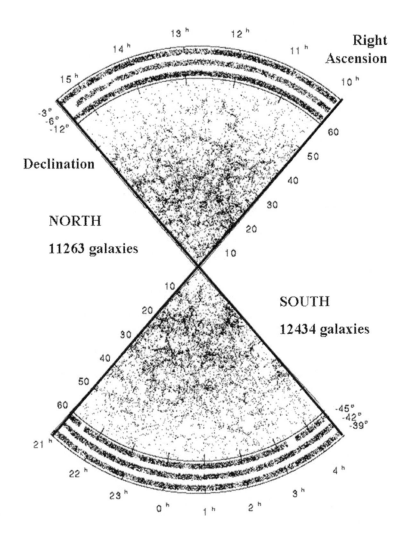

Right
Ascension

14 ʰ   13 ʰ   12 ʰ   11 ʰ   10 ʰ

15 ʰ

-3°
-6°
-12°

Declination

60

50

40

30

20

NORTH

11263 galaxies

10

10

20

SOUTH

30

12434 galaxies

40

50

-45°
-42°
-39°

60

21 ʰ

22 ʰ   4 ʰ

23 ʰ   3 ʰ

0 ʰ   1 ʰ   2 ʰ

JWST
(James Webb Space Telescope)

The James Webb Space Telescope is the largest, most powerful space telescope ever built. It will allow scientists to look at what our universe was like about 200 million years after the **Big Bang**. The telescope will be able to capture images of some of the first galaxies ever formed. It will also be able to observe objects in our Solar System from Mars outward, look inside dust clouds to see where new stars and planets are forming and examine the atmospheres of planets orbiting other stars.

The Webb telescope is as tall as a 3-story building and as long as a tennis court! It is so big that it has to fold origami-style to fit inside the rocket to launch. The telescope only unfolded, its sunshield first once it was in space.

The Webb telescope's cameras are sensitive to heat from the Sun. Just like you might wear a hat or a visor to block the Sun from your eyes, Webb has a sunshield to protect its instruments and mirrors. The telescope's sunshield is about the size of a tennis court. The temperature difference between the sun-facing and shaded sides of the telescope is more than 316^0 Celsius!

Space telescopes 'see' by using mirrors to collect and focus light from distant stars. The bigger the mirror, the more details the telescope can see. It's very difficult to launch a giant, heavy mirror into space. So, engineers gave the Webb telescope 18 smaller mirrors that fit together like a puzzle.

The James Webb Space Telescope launched on 25th December 2021, and the first pictures were received back on Earth on 11th July, 2022 from the telescope one million miles away.

These first pictures show thousands of galaxies, some of which formed nearly 13.2 billion years ago. They are seen in part because the James Webb Telescope targeted a cluster called SMACS 0723, which has a gravitational field so strong it magnifies the light of older, more distant galaxies.

NASA 2022

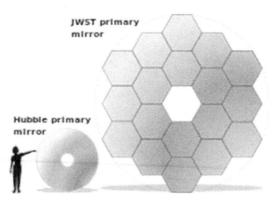

Comparison with Hubble primary mirror

Main mirror assembly from the front with primary mirrors attached, November 2016

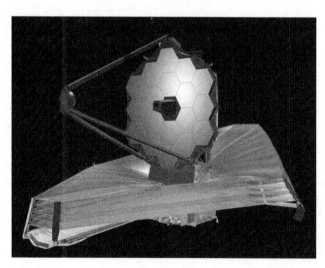

Three-quarter view of the top

Evolution of the Milky Way Galaxy

The Milky Way galaxy is a large spiral galaxy that hosts almost all of the stars that are seen in the night sky from Earth.

It is estimated that it could comprise approximately 400 billion stars that form a large disk.

300,000 Million years after the Big Bang

The history of the Milky Way galaxy is believed to have started as early as 300,000 million years after the Big Bang when enormous clouds of gas and dust came together due to the force of gravity.

To understand the history of the Milky Way galaxy, astronomers looked at the earliest stars of the galaxy which were composed mainly of hydrogen and helium, the most common elements in the Universe.

They were able to catalogue 42 ancient stars that are known as **ultra metal-poor stars**. Based on the classical story of the Milky Way galaxy, these stars should be swarming throughout the halo, and those stars in the disk should be contaminated with carbon and oxygen.

Researchers have found that half of the stars in the inner 60,000 light-years of the halo came from a collision of another galaxy that boosted the original mass of the Milky Way by 10%.

It appears that the incoming galaxy, '**Gaia-Enceladus**', collided with the **Milky Way** approximately 10 billion years ago and that the two disks in the Milky Way galaxy might have formed two parts, namely the thin and dark disks, because of this collision.

There is, however, evidence of other mergers which have been spotted in bundles of stars, called *globular clusters*.

13 Billion Years Ago

The Milky Way is an immense, flat, spiral galaxy surrounded by a massive **halo of stars** and **dark matter**. The disk of stars, gas, and dust in which the Sun resides is fully 120,000 light years across; an immense distance on terrestrial scales. In the middle of the disk is the central bulge, a lozenge-shaped hub of stars.

The Milky Way appears as flattened disk with spiral arms and a central bulge, a *halo*, and more than 150 globular clusters. The location of the Sun is about halfway out on one of its spiral arms.

It is estimated that stars within the Milky Way galaxy's 'thick disc' began generating 13 billion years ago, roughly 2 billion years sooner than expected, and just 0.8 billion years after the Big Bang, according to the ESA.

Stellar objects may have filled the thick disk and the stellar halo surrounding the entire galaxy with stars following the galactic collision with **Gaia-Enceladus**. The thin disk did not appear in the next great wave of star formation, which contained the Sun, for another 5 to 6 billion years.

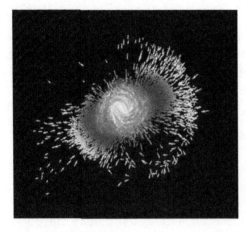

Artist's impression of debris of the Gaia-Enceladus galaxy.

*Surrounding arrows represent the positions and motions of stars originating from **Gaia-Enceladus** in a simulation of a galactic merger with the Milky Way with characteristics similar to those implied by Gaia satellite data.*

When the Universe was young it had almost no heavy elements like calcium and iron in it. Those were created in massive stars later, which then went *supernova* and seeded newly forming stars with those elements. Measuring the composition of a star can then be used to determine its age by comparing it to well-tested physical models of how stars evolve over time.

The Milky Way structure consists of a central bulge, a wide, flat disk, and a huge halo of stars surrounding it all. The disk actually has two components, a thin disk roughly 1,000 light-years through, and a thick disk roughly twice that.

7 Billion Years Ago

The thin disk is very roughly 1,000 light-years top-to-bottom and the thick disk a little more than twice that. The thick disk contains older stars in general, and the thin disk younger ones. It has been thought for some time that the thick disk formed roughly 11 billion years ago, a bit less than 3 billion years after the Big Bang.

64

New research shows, however, that the thick disk is much older than that. It started forming 13 billion years ago, less than a billion years after the Big Bang. The process of star formation continued for 6 billion years.

If this is so, then the thick disk started forming immediately, peaking around 11 billion years ago. This is also the same time that **Gaia-Enceladus**, collided with the **Milky Way.**

The disk then settled down, collisions of gas clouds in the disk caused them to migrate closer to the galactic midplane (an imaginary horizontal line cutting the Milky Way in two that defines galactic north and south) forming the thin disk. This material then underwent star formation, the second episode in the galaxy's stellar birth history. The Sun formed from this material in the thin disk, very close to the galactic midplane, and which is around 55 light-years to the north of that line.

The Sun formed in the aftermath of that galactic collision, which affected the thick disk and in part created the thin disk with the same material that formed the planets, and Earth together with all the constituents of life on it.

Using NASA's Kepler spacecraft, managed by NASA Ames Research Centre, astronomers have found Earth-sized planets orbiting distant stars.

The research team found that 50 percent of all stars have a planet of Earth-size or larger in a close orbit.

By adding larger planets detected in wider orbits up to the orbital distance of the Earth, this number increases to 70 percent. *NASA 2013*

The Milky Way in Space

As is typical for spiral galaxies, the *orbital speed* of most stars in the Milky Way does not depend strongly on their distance from the centre.
Away from the central bulge or outer rim, the typical stellar orbital speed is between **210 ± 10 km/s**.

Due to relativity, the velocity of the Milky Way varies when compared with different objects in space. The Milky Way and Andromeda galaxy, for example, are approaching one another with a velocity of about **130 km/s**. The Milky Way and its neighbours are moving at **600 km/s** in the direction of the constellation Hydra.

But the Milky Way also moves through space within the cluster of galaxies of which it is a member and this cluster in turn moves through space towards yet another larger cluster of galaxies. Relative to the Universe, the Milky Way galaxy is moving at a speed of approximately **590 km/s** in the same direction that the constellations of Virgo and Leo lay relative to the Earth. It is also moving at approximately **100 km/s** relative to the centre of mass of the Local Group. In comparison, the Earth moves around the Sun at the rate of **30 km/s**.

At its best it is bewildering, but the velocity of the Milky Way galaxy is not a single number but its value is **relative to the velocity of other objects**.

The motion of galaxies is determined from an apparent change in the colour of light they emit. There are gaps within the spectra of the light emerging from every galaxy. These gaps, called *absorption lines*, are not located in the spectra at random. The patterns in the missing wavelengths tell us something about the elements present in the stars. Each element has its own specific set of absorption lines.

When a star or group of stars within a galaxy are moving relative to Earth, these lines get shifted from their usual location in the spectra. When a galaxy is moving towards Earth, these lines get shifted toward the blue end of the spectrum and when a galaxy is moving away they get shifted toward the red end.
The amount of shift can be used to determine speed. The greater the shift, the faster the galaxy is moving relative to Earth.

The point towards which all stars and galaxies appear to be headed is called 'The Great Attractor'. Whereas the Milky Way galaxy contains the equivalent of 10^{11} solar masses, the Great Attractor is estimated to be on the scale of 10^{17} solar masses, a million times heavier than the Milky Way.

The Milky Way galaxy, along with everything else in the Universe, is moving through space.

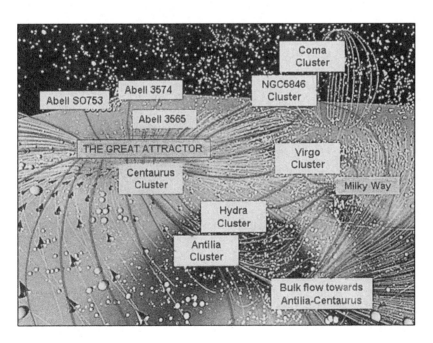

Therefore, the Earth moves around the Sun, the Sun in turn moves around the Milky Way and the Milky Way, as part of the Local Group, is moving relative to the Cosmic Microwave Background (CMB) radiation.

Earth rotates once in every 24 hour (*the actual value is 23 hours 56 minutes and 4 seconds!*) with respect to the Sun. At the equator, the circumference of the Earth is **40,075 km.** So the speed at which the Earth is spinning is about **1,670 km/h**.

The Earth's orbit around the Sun is elliptical, but for the sake of simplicity it is easier for the following example to consider it to be circular. So Earth's orbit is the circumference of a circle.

According to the International Astronomers Union, the mean distance from Earth to the Sun, called an *astronomical unit* (AU) is 149,597,870 km. That is the radius (*r*).

The circumference of a circle is $2\pi r$.
So, in one year, Earth travels:

$$2\pi r = 2 \cdot 3.14 \cdot 149{,}597{,}870 \text{ km}$$
$$= 939{,}474{,}624 \text{ km} \approx 9.395 \times 10^8 \text{ km.}$$

or $\quad 9.395 \times 10^8$ km / 365.25 = **2,572,141 km/day**
$\quad\quad\quad$ 2,572,141 / 24 = **107,173 km/hour**

So therefore Earth travels approximately **2.6 million km/day** or **107 thousand km/hour** in its path around the Sun. The entire Solar System orbits the centre of the Milky Way galaxy, and the Solar System orbits it at about **756,000 km/hour**.

The Milky Way galaxy is not a truly massive galaxy (Andromeda galaxy contains 1,000 billion stars compared to Milky Way's estimated 400 billion), but it still takes between **225 and 250 million years** for the Solar System to complete one passage around the galaxy's centre.

Evolution of the Solar System

The Solar System formed 4.568 billion years ago from the gravitational collapse of a region within a large molecular cloud.

This initial cloud was likely several light-years across and probably birthed several stars. As is typical of molecular clouds, this one consisted mostly of hydrogen, with some helium, and small amounts of heavier elements fused by previous generations of stars.

Most of the planets in the Solar System have secondary systems of their own, being orbited by planetary objects called natural satellites, or moons (two of which, Titan and Ganymede, are larger than the planet Mercury).

Pre-Solar System

Billions of years before formation of the Solar System

Over 4.6 Billion years ago

Previous generation of stars live and die, injecting heavy elements into the **interstellar medium** out of which the Solar System formed.

Interstellar medium. University of Oregon.

~50 million years before formation of the Solar System

4.6 Billion years ago

If the Solar System was formed in **an Orion nebula-like star-forming region**, the most massive stars would be formed, live their lives, die, and explode in supernova.

One particular supernova, called the *primal supernova*, possibly triggered the formation of the Solar System.

Deep infrared view of Orion Nebula star-forming region

Formation of the Sun

0-10,000 million years since formation of the Solar System

4.5 Billion years ago

Pre-solar nebula forms and begins to collapse.

Sun begins to form.

Sun is a **T Tauri protostar.**

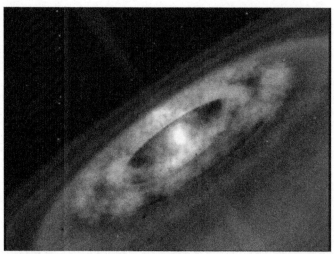

Artist's impression of a T Tauri star with a circumstellar accretion disc.

It is thought that the active magnetic fields and strong solar wind of Alfvén waves of T Tauri stars are one means by which angular momentum gets transferred from the star to the protoplanetary disc. A T Tauri stage for the Solar System would be one means by which the angular momentum of the contracting Sun was transferred to the protoplanetary disc and hence, eventually to the planets.

100,000 – 10 million years since formation of the Solar System

4.6 - 4.5 Billion years ago

Gas in the protoplanetary disc has been blown away, and outer planet formation is likely complete.

Terrestrial planets and the Moon form.
Giant impacts occur. Initial water delivered to Earth.

Main Sequence

50 million years since formation of the Solar System

4.5 - 4.4 Billion years ago

Sun becomes a **main-sequence** star.

Oldest known rocks on the Earth formed.

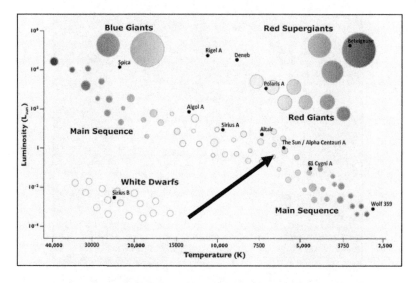

*The **Hertzsprung–Russell diagram**, is a scatter plot of stars which shows the relationship between the stars' absolute magnitudes or luminosities versus their stellar classifications or effective temperatures. It can be seen that most of the stars form along the '**main sequence**', the Sun being arrowed in the above diagram.*

500 - 600 million years since formation of the Solar System

4.0 – 4.1 Billion years ago

Resonance in Jupiter and Saturn's orbits moves Neptune out into the Kuiper belt.

Late Heavy Bombardment occurs in the inner Solar System.

Artist's impression of the Moon during the Late Heavy Bombardment (above) and today (below) Australian National University   CC BY-SA 3.0

800 million years since formation of the Solar System

3.8 Billion years ago

Oldest known life on Earth.

Oort Cloud reaches maximum.

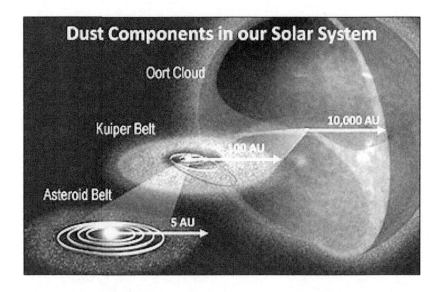

Titius-Bode Law

The **Titius-Bode Law** is a formulaic prediction of spacing between planets in any given solar system. The formula suggests that, extending outward, each planet should be approximately twice as far from the Sun as the one before. The hypothesis correctly anticipated the orbits of Ceres (in the Asteroid Belt) and Uranus, but failed as a predictor of Neptune's orbit.

The law predicts planets will be present at specific distances in astronomical units, which can be compared to the observed data for the planets and two dwarf planets in the Solar System.

m	k	T–B rule distance (AU)	Planet	Semi-major axis (AU)	Deviation from prediction
	0	0.4	Mercury	0.39	−3.23%
0	1	0.7	Venus	0.72	+3.33%
1	2	1.0	Earth	1.00	0.00%
2	4	1.6	Mars	1.52	−4.77%
3	8	2.8	Ceres	2.77	−1.16%
4	16	5.2	Jupiter	5.20	+0.05%
5	32	10.0	Saturn	9.58	−4.42%
6	64	19.6	Uranus	19.22	−1.95%
–	–	–	Neptune	30.07	–
7	128	38.8	Pluto	39.48	+1.02%

Later work by Mary Adele Blagg significantly corrected the original formula, and made predictions that were subsequently validated by new discoveries and observations. It is these reformulations that offer *'the best phenomenological representations of distances with which to investigate the theoretical significance of Titius-Bode type laws'*.

Johann Daniel Titius (1729–1796)

Johann Elert Bode (1747–1826

$$a = 4 + x$$

where x = 0, 3, 6, 12, 24, 48, 96, 192 ....

alternatively,

$$a = 4 + 3 \times 2^n$$

where n = ∞, 0, 1, 2, 3, 4 .....

Later, in Bragg's formulation, the law for the Solar System was better represented by a progression in **1.7275** and not 2.

Planets			
Planet	n	Distance	Blagg Law
Mercury	-2	0.387	0.387
Venus	-1	0.723	0.723
Earth	0	1.000	1.000
Mars	1	1.524	1.524
Vesta	2	2.361	2.67
Juno	2	2.670	2.67
Pallas	2	2.767	2.67
Ceres	2	2.767	2.67
Jupiter	3	5.203	5.200
Saturn	4	9.546	9.550
Uranus	5	19.20	19.23
Neptune	6	30.07	30.13
Pluto	7	(39.5)	41.8

Geological Time Scale

The **Geologic Time Scale** is a system used by scientists to describe Earth's history in terms of major geological or paleontological events, such as the formation of a new rock layer or the appearance or demise of certain life forms.

'The Persistence of Memory', Dali

Geologic time spans are divided into units and subunits, the largest of which are eons. Eons are divided into eras, which are further divided into periods, epochs, and ages. Geologic dating is **extremely imprecise**. For example, although the date listed for the beginning of the Ordovician period is 485 million years ago, it is actually 485.4 with an uncertainty (plus or minus) of 1.9 million years.

Geologic dating allows scientists to better understand ancient history, including the evolution of plant and animal life from single-celled organisms to dinosaurs to primates to early humans. It also helps them learn more about how human activity has transformed the planet.

The dates shown on this **Geologic Time Scale** were specified by the International Commission on Stratigraphy in 2015.

Of course, these geologic units are not equal in length. Eons, Eras, and Periods are usually separated by a significant geologic event and are unique in their climate, landscape, and biodiversity.

The Cenozoic era, for example, is known as the 'Age of Mammals', The Carboniferous period, on the other hand, is named for the large coal beds that were formed during this time ('carboniferous' means coal-bearing). The Cryogenian period, as its name suggests, was a time of great glaciations.

Eon	Era	Period	Epoch	Date (Mya)
Hadean*				4560 - 3600
Archean				
	Paleoarchean			3600 - 3400
	Mesoarchean			3400 - 3000
	Neoarchean			3000 - 2500
Proterzoic				
	Paleoproterozoic			
		Siderian		2500 - 2300
		Rhyacian		2300 - 2050
		Orosirian		2050 - 1800
		Statherian		1800 - 1600
	Mesoproterozoic			
		Calymmian		1600 - 1400
		Ectasian		1400 - 1200
		Stenian		1200 - 0900
	Neoproterozoic			
		Tonian		0900 - 0700
		Cryogenian		0720 - 0835
		Ediacaran		0835 - 0540
Phanerozoic				
	Paleozoic			
		Cambrian		0540 - 0485
		Ordocvician		0485 - 0444
		Silurian		0444 - 0419
		Devonian		0419 - 0359
		Carboniferous		
			Mississsippian	0359 - 0323
			Pennsylvanian	0323 - 0299
		Permian		0299 - 0248
	Mesozoic			
		Triassic		0248 - 0201
		Jurassic		0201 - 0145
		Cretaceous		0145 - 0066
	Cenozoic			
		Paleogene		
			Paleocene	0066 - 0058
			Eocene	0058 - 0036
			Oligocene	0036 - 0025
		Neogene		
			Miocene	0025 - 0013
			Pliocene	0013 - 0002
		Quaternary		
			Pleistocene	0002 - 000.1
			Holocene	000.1 - Present

Era	Period	Epoch	Mya
Cenozoic	Quarternary	Holocene	0.01
		Pleistocene	1.8
	Neogene	Pliocene	5.3
		Miocene	23.8
	Paleogene	Oligocene	33.7
		Eocene	54.8
		Paleocene	66.0
Mesozoic	Cretaceous		
			144
	Jurassic		
			206
	Triassic		
			246
Paleozoic	Permian		
			290
	Carboniferous	Pennsylvanian	
			323
		Mississippian	
			354
	Devonian		
			417
	Silurian		
			443
	Ordovician		
			490
	Cambrian		
			540
Precambrian			

Geological Eons

Eon	Era	Mya
Phanerozoic	Cenozoic	66
	Mesozoic	248
	Paleozoic	540
Precambrian — Proterozoic	Neoproterozoic	900
	Mesoproterozoic	1600
	Paleoproterozoic	2500
Precambrian — Archean	Neoarchean	3000
	Mesoarchean	3400
	Paleoarchean	3600
Precambrian — Hadean		4560

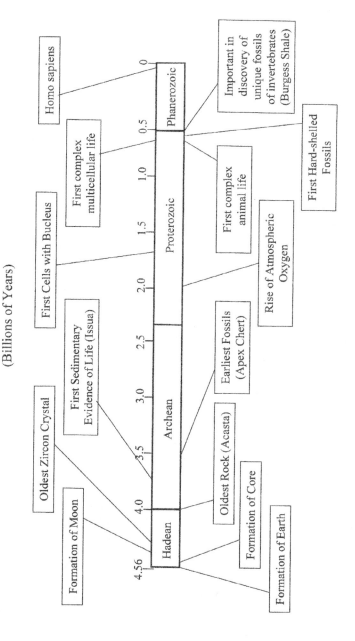

Key Events in Geological Timeline
(Billions of Years)

Hadean Eon (4.56 to 3.6 Ga)

Hadean is not strictly an Eon insofar as it was the period of the formation of the Earth from its birth at the start as an unsettled body to one which was ordered and reasonably stable with oceans and an atmosphere. For convenience, Hadean is regarded here as an Eon.

It follows therefore that the oldest of the geologic eons here is the Hadean, which began about 4.56 billion years ago with the formation of Earth and ended about 3.6 billion years ago with the appearance of the first single-celled organisms. This eon is named after Hades, the Greek god of the underworld, and during this period the Earth was extremely hot. Although water was present at this time, the heat would have boiled it away into steam. Oceans as we know them today did not appear until the Earth's crust began to cool many years later.

When the material forming the Earth coalesced and melted, it organized itself into layers with dense materials at the core and less dense compounds closer to the surface.

The gases comprising the atmosphere formed the outermost layer and had a composition similar to that of the gases of the condensing planetary nebula.

During the Hadean, the Earth's surface consisted of molten rock, a magma ocean, and water existed only as steam in the atmosphere.

It is hypothesised that around 4.45 Ga, the Earth experienced a violent collision with a planetoid called **Theia** that was about the size of Mars. It is theorized that this collision added extra mass to the Earth, but a portion of the impact debris went into orbit and accreted to form the Moon. (*In Greek mythology, Theia was the name of a titaness who was the mother of Selene, the goddess of the Moon, which parallels the planetoid Theia's collision with the early Earth*).

Some scientists have proposed that this giant impact blasted away into space Earth's entire atmosphere, including much of the water, and that the atmosphere and water were subsequently replenished by volcanic out gassing and impacts from asteroids and comets.

A problem with this proposal is that the ratio of deuterium to hydrogen (D/H) for comets is very different from what is found in the Earth's oceans, so comets are not a likely source for all of Earth's water. Also, volcanic emissions do not have much nitrogen, so it is unlikely that volcanism provided the nitrogen in our current atmosphere. While it is true that a great collision would have sent much of the atmosphere into space, most of it would have remained within the Earth's gravitational sphere of influence and could have been recaptured by the Earth as the debris from the giant impact cooled and was partitioned between the Earth and the newly formed Moon giving both a similar chemical composition.

After the hydrogen and helium had escaped, Earth's Hadean atmosphere was left with methane, ammonia, water vapour, and small percentages of nitrogen and carbon dioxide.

A cataclysmic meteorite bombardment around 3.9 Ga kept much of the Earth's surface in the molten state, and the incoming impactors may well have brought additional water, methane, ammonia, hydrogen sulphide and other gases that supplemented the atmosphere.

The high surface temperature of the Earth during the Hadean favoured the depletion of atmospheric methane through the endothermic reaction of methane with the steam in the atmosphere (3). Reactions such as this require high temperatures of approximately 800°C to 1100°C which would have been common in the hot crust and magma lakes of the Hadean Earth.

$$CH_4 + H_2O^{steam} \longrightarrow CO + 3H_2 \quad \Delta H = -206 \text{ kJ/mol} \quad (1)$$
$$CO + H_2O^{steam} \longrightarrow CO_2 + H_2 \quad \Delta H = -41 \text{ kJ/mol} \quad (2)$$

$$CH_4 + 2H_2O^{steam} \longrightarrow CO_2 + 4H_2 \quad \Delta H = 165 \text{ kJ/mol} \quad (3)$$

Much of the resulting carbon monoxide in (1) would readily combine with metals to form carbonyl compounds.

The Hadean was too hot for liquid water to condense on the surface of the Earth, but water vapour would have been able to condense at high altitude in the atmosphere and produce rain that evaporated quickly as it fell when it approached the ground.

Towards the end of the Hadean, volcanic activity started increasing the percentage of carbon dioxide in the atmosphere. The Earth's surface changed from molten lava to solid rock, and liquid water started to accumulate on the surface.

Archean Eon   (3.6 to 2.5 Ga)

The next geologic eon, the Archean, began about 3.6 billion years ago. During this period, the cooling of the Earth's crust allowed for the formation of the first oceans and continents. The amount of water vapour in the atmosphere decreased as water started condensing in liquid form.

Continuous rainfall for millions of years led to the build-up of the oceans. As steam condensed into water, the atmospheric pressure of the Earth became lower, and the water started dissolving gases like ammonia and removed them from the atmosphere creating ammonium compounds, amines and other nitrogen-containing substances suitable for the origin of life.

Scientists are not exactly sure what these continents looked like since there is so little evidence from the period. However, some are of the opinion that the first landmass on Earth was a **supercontinent** known as **Ur**. Others think it was a supercontinent known as **Vaalbara**   (*refer to 13. Evolution of Supercontinents*).

It is thought that the first single-celled life forms developed during the Archean. These tiny microbes left their mark in layered rocks known as *Stromatolites*, some of which are nearly 3.5 billion years old such as these pictured here in Australia.

Unlike the Hadean, the Archean is divided into eras: the Eoarchean, Paleoarchean, Mesoarchean, and Neoarchean. The Neoarchean, which began about 2.8 billion years ago, was the era in which oxygenic photosynthesis began.

This process, performed by algae and other micro-organisms, caused oxygen molecules in water to be released into the atmosphere. Prior to oxygenic photosynthesis, Earth's atmosphere had no free oxygen, a huge impediment to the evolution of life.

The condensation of water with gases such as sulphur dioxide produced **acid rain** that created new minerals on the Earth's surface. Volcanic carbon dioxide peaked during the Archean and started to decrease through the formation of carbonate minerals that resulted from reactions of metals with the carbonic acid generated from carbon dioxide and water.

$$NH_3 + H_2O \rightarrow NH_4^+ + OH^-$$
$$CO_2 + H_2O \rightarrow H_2CO_3$$
carbonic acid

Microfossils of sulphur-metabolizing cells have been found in 3.4 Ga rocks, and it is known that the first aquatic photosynthetic organisms originated around 3.5 Ga. The oxygen produced by *cyano-bacteria* (otherwise known as *blue-green algae*) during the Archean reacted with the metal ions in the anoxic sea.

Billions of years would pass before the photosynthetic micro-organisms could eventually change the composition of the atmosphere. By the middle of the Archean, the Earth had cooled enough so that most of the water vapour in the atmosphere had condensed as water, and the Earth had its first days without clouds.

At that time the atmosphere comprised:

carbon dioxide	(CO_2)	15%
methane	(CH_4)	only minimal levels
ammonia	(NH_3)	only minimal levels
nitrogen	(N)	75%
oxygen	(O)	negligible

In essence, most of the original components of the atmosphere had escaped, precipitated as liquids or reacted chemically to form solid compounds. The volcanic activity and the **photosynthetic bacteria** had become the major factors influencing the Earth's atmospheric composition.

The scene had now been set for the greatest show on Earth, the ability for **amino acids** to be produced from the basic gases now present in the atmosphere.

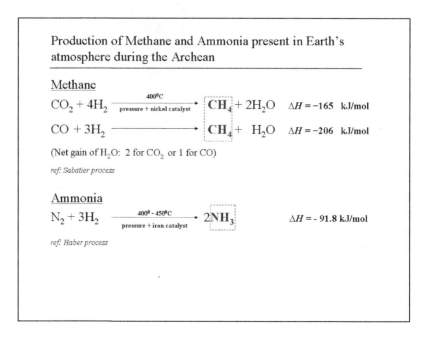

Production of Methane and Ammonia present in Earth's atmosphere during the Archean

Methane

$$CO_2 + 4H_2 \xrightarrow[\text{pressure + nickel catalyst}]{400^\circ C} CH_4 + 2H_2O \quad \Delta H = -165 \text{ kJ/mol}$$

$$CO + 3H_2 \longrightarrow CH_4 + H_2O \quad \Delta H = -206 \text{ kJ/mol}$$

(Net gain of H_2O: 2 for CO_2 or 1 for CO)

ref: Sabatier process

Ammonia

$$N_2 + 3H_2 \xrightarrow[\text{pressure + iron catalyst}]{400^\circ - 450^\circ C} 2NH_3 \quad \Delta H = -91.8 \text{ kJ/mol}$$

ref: Haber process

Carbon dioxide began to be taken up in the water 'sink' which was now forming over wide expanses of the newly formed seas. But more water was to be produced, not necessarily from the bombardment of meteoroids from outer space, or the volcanic rocks, but from the basic components which had now been formed.

As Miller and Urey demonstrated in their epic experiment of 1962, this was not only feasible, but possible.

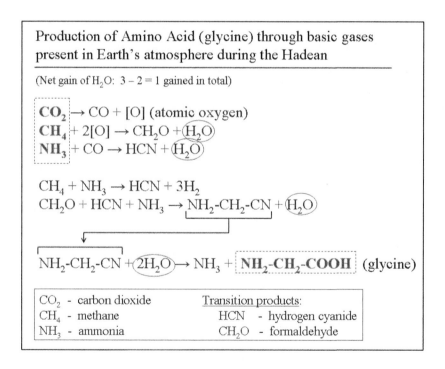

Production of Amino Acid (glycine) through basic gases present in Earth's atmosphere during the Hadean

(Net gain of H_2O: $3 - 2 = 1$ gained in total)

$CO_2 \rightarrow CO + [O]$ (atomic oxygen)
$CH_4 + 2[O] \rightarrow CH_2O + H_2O$
$NH_3 + CO \rightarrow HCN + H_2O$

$CH_4 + NH_3 \rightarrow HCN + 3H_2$
$CH_2O + HCN + NH_3 \rightarrow NH_2\text{-}CH_2\text{-}CN + H_2O$

$NH_2\text{-}CH_2\text{-}CN + 2H_2O \rightarrow NH_3 + NH_2\text{-}CH_2\text{-}COOH$ (glycine)

CO_2 - carbon dioxide	Transition products:
CH_4 - methane	HCN - hydrogen cyanide
NH_3 - ammonia	CH_2O - formaldehyde

The Miller-Urey Experiment

The **Miller–Urey experiment** was a chemical experiment that simulated the conditions thought at the time (1952) to be present on the early Earth and tested the chemical origin of life under those conditions.

After Miller's death in 2007, scientists examining sealed vials preserved from the original experiments were able to show that there were actually **well over 20 different amino acids** produced in Miller's original experiments. That is considerably more than what Miller originally reported, and **more than the 20 that naturally occur in the genetic code**.

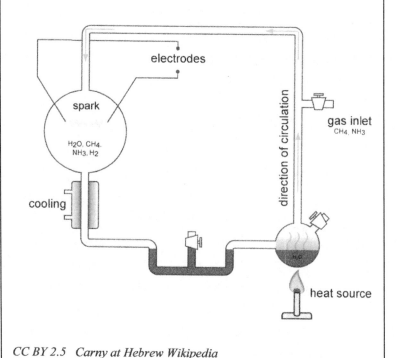

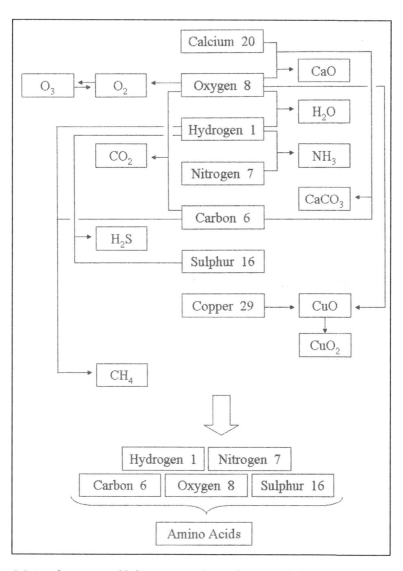

*Main elements of life, essential products and those essential
for most Amino Acids*

Proterozoic Eon   (2.5 to 0.54 Ga)

The Proterozoic began about 2.5 billion years ago and ended about 500 million years ago when the first complex life-forms appeared. During this time, the **Great Oxygenation Event** transformed the Earth's atmosphere, allowing for the evolution of aerobic organisms. The Proterozoic was also the eon in which the Earth's first glaciers formed. Some scientists even consider that during the Neoproterozoic, about 650 million years ago, the surface of the Earth became frozen.

The first multicellular organisms developed during this eon, including early forms of algae. Fossils from this time are very small. Some of the most notable are the Gabon macrofossils, which were discovered in Gabon, West Africa. The fossils include flattened disks up to 17 centimetres long.

Unicellular life proliferated and anaerobic microbial life thrived in a planet with little oxygen. Anaerobic organisms obtained their energy in various ways. Methanogens combined hydrogen and carbon dioxide to produce methane and water:

$$CO_2 + 4H_2 \longrightarrow CH_4 + 2H_2O$$

Sulphate producing bacteria combined methane to produce sulphate radicals:

$$CH_4 + SO_4^- \longrightarrow HCO_3^- + HS^- + H_2O$$

Other organisms capable of photosynthesis started to use one of three different variations (C3 – the most common), C4 and CAM to convert the energy of sunlight and abundant carbon dioxide and water into carbohydrates and oxygen, which gas as has already been stated was deadly to the early anaerobes.

$$6CO_2 + 6H_2O \longrightarrow C_6H_{12}O_6 + 6O_2 \qquad \textbf{(variation C3)}$$
carbohydrate

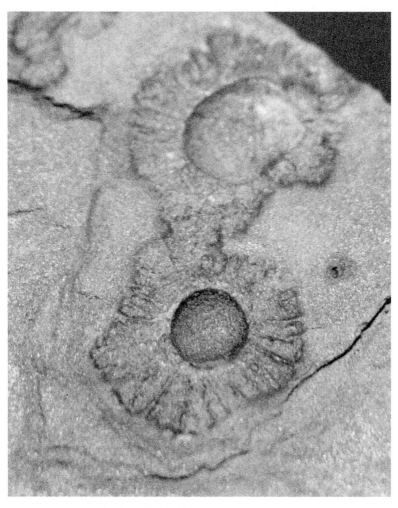

The **Gabon macrofossils** also known as **Francevillian biota** is a group of 2.1-billion-year-old Palaeoproterozoic, macroscopic organisms known from fossils found in Gabon The fossils are postulated to be evidence of the earliest form of multicellular life.

Unicellular organism

A **unicellular organism** is an organism that consists of a single cell, unlike a multicellular organism that consists of multiple cells.

Organisms fall into two general categories: *prokaryotic* organisms and *eukaryotic* organisms.

All prokaryotes are unicellular and are classified into bacteria and archaea. Many eukaryotes are multicellular, but some are unicellular such as protozoa, unicellular algae, and unicellular fungi.

Unicellular organisms are thought to be the oldest form of life, with early *protocells (i.e. 'coacervate')* possibly emerging 3.8–4.0 billion years ago.

Valonia ventricosa is a species of alga with a diameter that ranges typically from 1 to 4 centimetres is among the largest unicellular species.

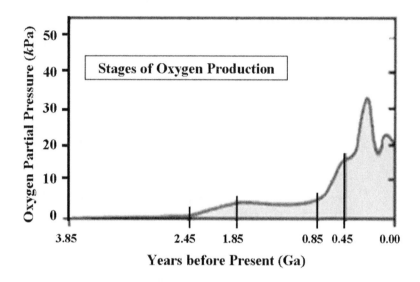

By the first quarter of the Proterozoic, the Sun had become brighter and its luminosity had increased to 85% of the present level. By this time, most of the carbon dioxide had been depleted from the atmosphere, leaving nitrogen as the main atmospheric gas with a small percentage of oxygen.

Nitrogen gas (N_2), which is quite chemically inert, had been a small percentage of the Earth's atmosphere during the Hadean and Archean, but it became the major component of the atmosphere during the Proterozoic once all the other gases were gone.

The Earth's surface and seas contained great quantities of iron that readily combined with oxygen to produce iron oxides. From the beginning of the Proterozoic to 1.85 Ga, atmospheric oxygen levels rose as the rate of photosynthesis increased significantly. Shallow seas became partially oxygenated, but the deep oceans continued to be anoxic.

Although photosynthetic organisms had been releasing oxygen since Archean times, the oxygen levels could not build up in the atmosphere because the oxygen was being depleted by the oxidation of metals and by the oxidation of methane to yield carbon dioxide and water in the presence of ultraviolet (UV) radiation.

$$4Fe + 3\,O_2 \longrightarrow 2Fe_2O_3$$
Oxidation of metallic iron to form iron (III) oxide

$$CH_4 + 2O_2 \longrightarrow CO_2 + 2H_2O$$
Oxidation of methane

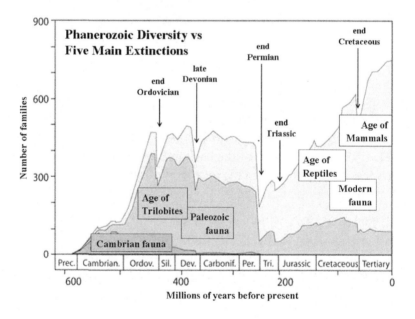

The cooling of the Earth during the Proterozoic stabilized the land masses and reduced the volcanic out-gassing of carbon dioxide. Methane and carbon dioxide are 'greenhouse gases', their decrease in the atmosphere may have contributed to the 'Huronian glaciation' that lasted from 2.4 Ga to 2.1 Ga.

The cold temperature sequestered additional methane from the atmosphere by forming **methane clathrate $(CH_4)_4(H_2O)_{23}$**, a crystal structure of water similar to ice that traps a large amount of methane. An increased period of oxygen production occurred between 2.4 Ga and 2.0 Ga and is known as the **Great Oxidation Event** or **Oxygen Catastrophe**. The higher oxygen level created *banded iron formations* (BIF) by precipitating dissolved iron. The reaction of oxygen with iron in its reduced state (Fe^{2+}) continued to create BIF deposits of iron in its oxidized state (Fe^{3+}) until about 1.9 Ga whenever volcanic activity or crustal plate movements exposed unoxidized iron.

Additional oxygen continued to be consumed by oxidation of minerals on the Earth's crust, but enough free oxygen accumulated in the atmosphere to kill anaerobes near the Earth's surface thus creating an opportunity for the development of aerobic life forms.

Starting around 2.4 Ga, oxygen molecules migrated into the upper atmosphere and formed an **ozone layer**. This is a region in the stratosphere located between 15 to 35 km above the Earth's surface where oxygen molecules (O_2) are converted to ozone (O_3) by the Sun's ultraviolet rays.

The reverse conversion of ozone back to oxygen releases heat. The ozone layer basically absorbs high-energy ultraviolet radiation and converts it to heat. The high energy UV light is dangerous for life because it can cause mutations in DNA sequences.

The atmospheric composition was very steady between 1.85 Ga to 0.85 Ga. During this time, Earth's atmosphere had approximately 10% oxygen.

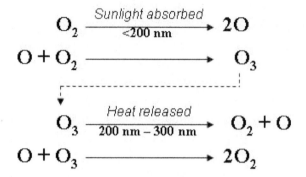

(Net loss of one molecule of ozone per cycle)

Photosynthetic organisms were still producing oxygen at a high rate, but the reaction of oxygen with dissolved minerals in the deep oceans and with rock and clay on the Earth's surface did not allow atmospheric oxygen levels to increase.

By 0.85 Ga, the minerals in the sea and on land could not bind as much oxygen, and the excess oxygen began to accumulate in the atmosphere. With the increased oxygen levels and the protection of the ozone layer, organisms capable of aerobic respiration could now proliferate all over the surface of the Earth.

> The global exchange between ozone and oxygen is in the order of three million tonnes per day.

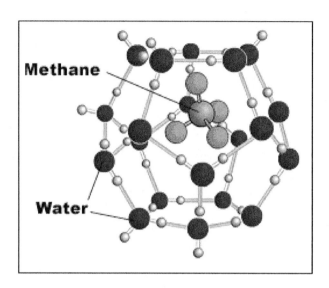

Methane Clathrate

Methane clathrate was originally thought to occur only in the outer regions of the Solar System, where temperatures are low and water ice is common, significant deposits of methane clathrate have been found under sediments on the ocean floors of the Earth. Methane hydrate is formed when hydrogen-bonded water and methane gas come into contact at high pressures and low temperatures in oceans.

103

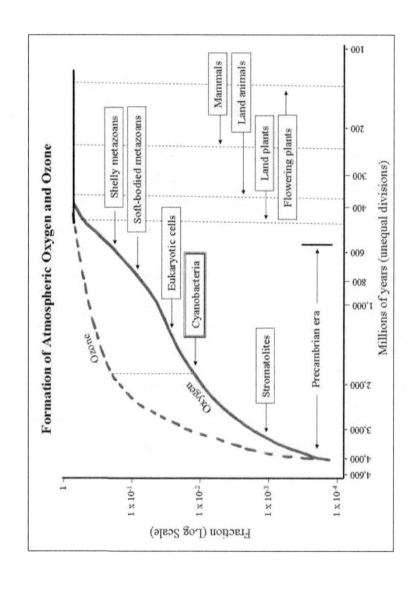

Formation of Atmospheric Oxygen and Ozone

Phanerozoic Eon   (0.54 Ga to present)

The most recent geologic eon is the Phanerozoic, which began about 540 million years ago. This eon is very distinct from the previous three—the Hadean, Archean, and Proterozoic - which are sometimes known as the Precambrian era. During the Cambrian, the earliest part of the Phanerozoic, the first complex organisms appeared. Vegetation covered the surface of the Earth, and oxygen accounted for 30% of the atmosphere.

Air enriched with so much oxygen allowed giant insects to develop and caused frequent forest fires set off by lightning. Most of the fauna was aquatic. The famous examples are *trilobites*, small *arthropods* (creatures with exoskeletons) whose distinct fossils are still being discovered today. During the Ordovician, fish, *cephalopods*, and corals first appeared. Over time, these creatures eventually evolved into amphibians and dinosaurs.

During the Mesozoic, which began about 248 million years ago, dinosaurs ruled the planet. These creatures were the largest to ever walk the Earth. Titanosaur, for example, grew up to 120 feet long, five times as long as an African elephant. The dinosaurs were eventually killed during the **K/Pg Extinction** which occurred 66 million years ago, an event that eliminated about 75% of all species that were alive on Earth at that time.

Following the Mesozoic was the Cenozoic, which began about 66 million years ago. This period is also known as the **'Age of Mammals'** as large mammals, following the extinction of the dinosaurs, became the dominant creatures on the planet.

In the process, mammals diversified into the many species still present on the Earth today, including *Homo habilis* and *Homo sapiens*.

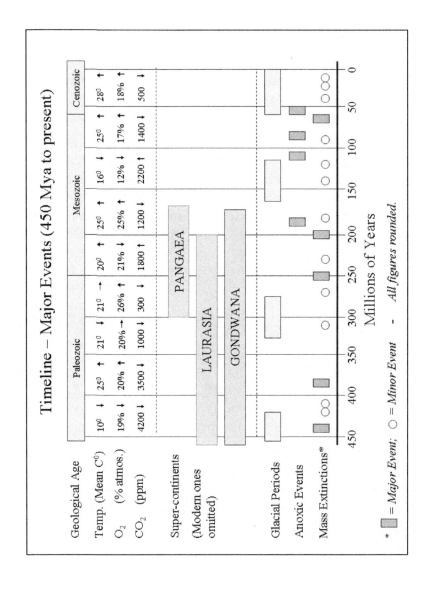

Timeline – Major Events (450 Mya to present)

These enormous changes to life on Earth have taken place over a period of time that, compared to geologic history, is relatively small. Human activity has transformed the planet. Some scientists have proposed a new epoch, the '**Anthropocene**' to describe this new period of life on Earth.

A great mass-extinction event occurred 250 million years ago (0.25 Ga) marking the boundary of the Permian and Triassic periods. Oxygen levels dropped progressively from 30% to 12%, and carbon dioxide levels reached about 2200 ppm (*refer to chart on previous page*).

This was Earth's worst mass extinction and it eliminated 96% of all species. The cause of this mass extinction is thought to have been a series of volcanic events in Siberia that lasted for about one million years releasing large volumes of carbon dioxide and gases containing sulphur, chlorine and fluorine.

By 228 million years ago, oxygen levels had risen to about 15% of the atmosphere, and the first dinosaurs appeared.

Oxygen levels continued to increase, and by the end-Cretaceous, 100 million years ago, oxygen had risen substantially. At this time, dinosaurs were well established and modern mammals and birds began to develop. For the last 100 million years, the percentage of oxygen has fluctuated to the present level of about 21% of the atmosphere.

Geological Periods

Era	Period	Epoch	Mya
Cenozoic	Quarternary	Holocene	0.01
		Pleistocene	1.8
	Neogene	Pliocene	5.3
		Miocene	23.8
	Paleogene	Oligocene	33.7
		Eocene	54.8
		Paleocene	66.0
Mesozoic	Cretaceous		
			144
	Jurassic		
			206
	Triassic		
			246
Paleozoic	Permian		
			290
	Carboniferous	Pennsylvanian	
			323
		Mississippian	
			354
	Devonian		
			417
	Silurian		
			443
	Ordovician		
			490
	Cambrian		
			540
Precambrian			

Precambrian Period

The **Precambrian** is not really a single unified time period ... it makes up roughly seven-eighths of the Earth's history. In other words, most of what Earth did, it was done during the Precambrian. Hence the most important events in biological history took place during this time. The Earth formed, **the first tectonic plates** began to move, **eukaryotic cells evolved**, the atmosphere became enriched in oxygen, and just before the end of this period complex multi-cellular organisms including the first animals evolved.

During the first part of the Precambrian - the **Achaean** - the atmosphere was markedly different from what we know today. It was a soup of methane, ammonia, and other gases which would be toxic to pretty much everything that now live on Earth. Our oldest fossils date to the Achaean, approximately 3.5 billion years ago, and consist of bacteria microfossils.

The second half of the Precambrian was the **Proterozoic**. Stable continents began to form over the next billion years, and the first abundant fossils of living organisms (mostly bacteria) appeared. By about 1.8 billion years ago eukaryotic cells began to enter the record, which is the first evidence of oxygen in the atmosphere.

Oxygen meant life for some, but disaster for some of the existing inhabitants.

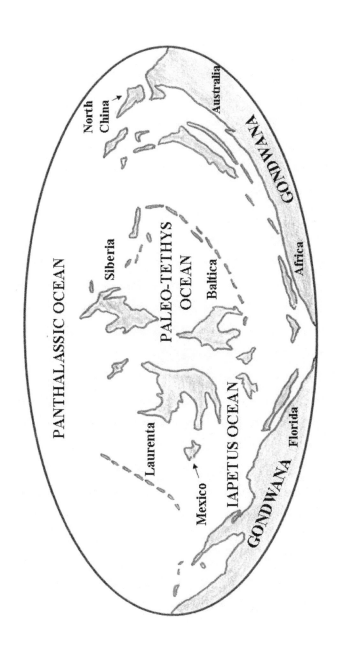

Phanerozoic (540 Mya)

Cambrian Period (540 to 490 Mya)

Eon	Era	Period	Date
Phanerozoic	Paleozoic	>> Cambrian	540 - 490
		Ordovician	490 - 443
		Silurian	443 - 417
		Devonian	417 - 354
		Carboniferous	354 - 290
		Permian	290 - 248

Coscinocyathus
Dictyonema
Helicionella
Laosciadia
Lingulelia
Olenus
Paradooxides

This was a time when most of the major groups of animals first appear in the fossil record. This event is sometimes called the '**Cambrian Explosion**', because of the relatively short time over which this diversity of life forms 'exploded'.

Whilst life began to flourish in the seas, though, the land was completely barren. It basically had a microbial '*crud*' that acted as a soil crust covering the land. Apart from some minor evidence that a few animals might have made land, the new continents (which had just formed during the break-up of the supercontinent **Pannotia**) resembled deserts with shallow seas at the margins. The seas were relatively warm, and for most of this era, there was no polar ice at all.

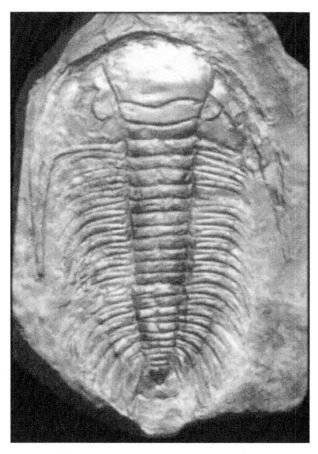

Paradoxides davidis (trilobite). Sam Gon III

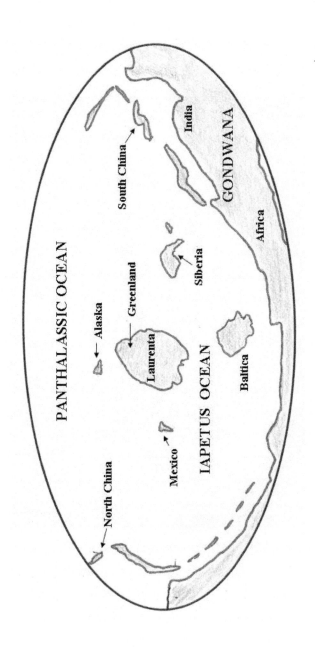

Late Cambrian (513 Mya)

Ordovician Period   (490 to 443 Mya)

Eon	Era	Period	Date
Phanerozoic	Paleozoic	Cambrian	540 - 490
		>> Ordovician	490 - 443
		Silurian	443 - 417
		Devonian	417 - 354
		Carboniferous	354 - 290
		Permian	290 - 248

Cyclonema
Didymorgaplus
Nicolella
Selenopeltis
Tretragraplus

During the Ordovician, most of the world's land was combined into the southern super-continent **Gondwana**. Throughout this period, Gondwana shifted towards the South Pole and much of it was submerged underwater. Because of this, the Ordovician is known for its diverse marine invertebrates, including *graptolites*, *trilobites*, *brachiopods*, and the *conodonts* (very early vertebrates). A typical marine community consisted of these animals, plus red and green algae, primitive fish, *cephalopods*, *corals*, *crinoids*, and *gastropods*. More recently, evidence has been found of tetrahedral spores that are similar to those of primitive land plants, suggesting that plants may have invaded the land at this time.

From the early to mid- part of this period, the weather was pleasantly warm and muggy.

However, when Gondwana finally finished moving in on the South Pole at the end of this time, massive glaciers formed causing shallow seas to drain and sea levels to drop. That was bad news for all the living organisms that really liked warm, shallow seas to live in. This is very likely what caused the mass extinctions that characterise the end of the Ordovician, in which 60% of all marine invertebrate genera and 25% of all families went extinct.

Selenopeltis buchi - Czech Republic National Museum (Prague)   CC BY-SA 3.0

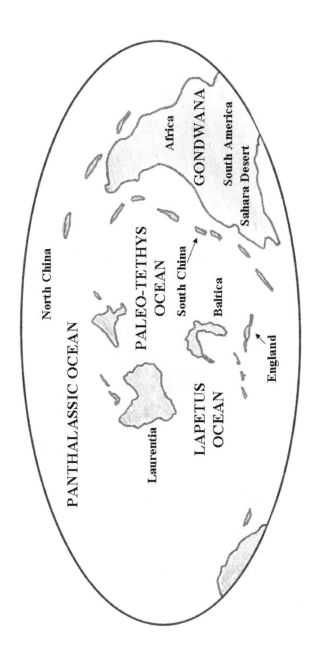

Middle Ordovician (458 Mya)

Silurian Period   (43 to 417 Mya)

Eon	Era	Period	Date
Phanerozoic	Paleozoic	Cambrian	540 - 490
		Ordovician	490 - 443
		>> Silurian	443 - 417
		Devonian	417 - 354
		Carboniferous	354 - 290
		Permian	290 - 248

Cyrtographus
Gissocrinus
Kodonophyllum
Platyschisma
Spirograptus
Trigonirhynchia

Thanks to the stabilization of the Earth's general climate, the Silurian ended the previous pattern of erratic climates. Because of this, the glaciers started to melt, which contributed to a major rise in the levels of larger seas. Coral reefs came about for the first time, and fish evolution became an ongoing event. The Silurian saw the rapid spread of jawless fish as well as the incredibly important appearances of both freshwater fish and first fish with jaws.

The Silurian is also the first period in Earth's history where there is solid evidence of life on land, including relatives of spiders and centipedes, and also the earliest fossils of vascular plants.

Spirograptus spiralis, sobre pizarra. Silúrico de Guadalajara.
by L. Fernández García   CC BY-SA 2.5 es

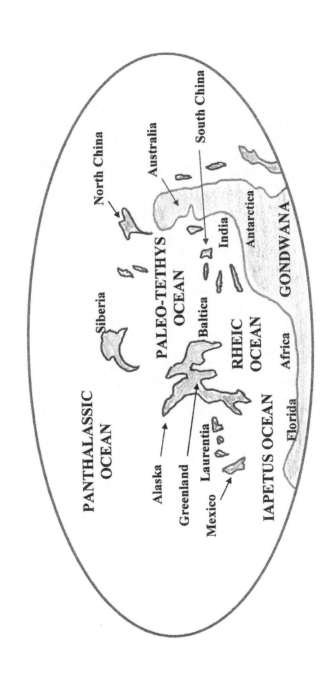

Middle Silurian (425 Mya)

Devonian Period (417 to 354 Mya)

Eon	Era	Period	Date
Phanerozoic	Paleozoic	Cambrian	540 - 490
		Ordovician	490 - 443
		Silurian	443 - 417
		>> Devonian	417 - 354
		Carboniferous	354 - 290
		Permian	290 - 248

Osteolepis
Pteraspis
Stringocephalus
Stromatapora

The oldest known vascular plants in the Northern Hemisphere are Devonian, the tallest being only a meter tall, but while small, diversity was on the rise. By the end of this period, ferns, horsetails and seed plants had appeared. Devonian plants did not have roots or leaves like the plants most common today, and many had no vascular tissue at all. There were so many new plants at this time that it is called the '**Devonian Explosion**'.

Two major animal groups were starting to really develop. The first land-living vertebrates appeared as did the first arthropods, including wingless insects and the earliest arachnids.

As for what the Earth itself looked like on its face, there were now three major continental masses: North America and Europe sat together near the equator, with a lot of their current land underwater.

The land masses of South America, Africa, Antarctica, India, and Australia dominated the southern hemisphere.

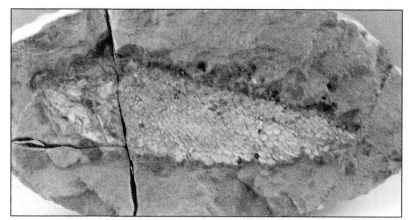

Osteolepis macrolepidotus AGASSIS, Scotland

Stromatapora

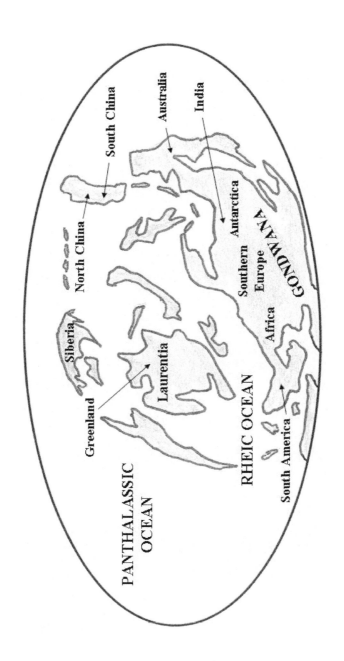

Early Devonian (390 Mya)

Carboniferous Period (354 to 290 Mya)

Eon	Era	Period	Date
Phanerozoic	Paleozoic	Cambrian	540 - 490
		Ordovician	490 - 443
		Silurian	443 - 417
		Devonian	417 - 354
		>> Carboniferous	354 - 290
		Permian	290 – 248

Cornuboniscus
Endothyranopsis
Lepidodendron
Palaeosmilia
Kugosochonetes
Xanacsnthus

One of the most important things that came out of the Carboniferous was the *'amniote egg'*, which allowed for the further exploitation of the land by certain vertebrates. The *'amniote egg'* let the ancestors of birds, mammals, and reptiles reproduce on land by protecting the embryo in fluid (amniotic fluid), preventing it from drying out. This was also a time of larger plants and the tree-fern. Milder temperatures caused a decrease in *lycopods* and large insects, and an increase in the number of these tree ferns. The plants from this time resemble the plants that live in tropical and mildly temperate areas today. Many of them lack growth rings, suggesting a uniform climate.

The presence of two large ice sheets at the southern pole was sucking up a huge amount of Earth's water, and because of this, the sea levels all over the world fluctuated. This led to another mass extinction, this time for shallow marine invertebrates.

It also caused the gradual decline of swamps and the increase in dry land habitat.

Meanwhile, the continents were busy colliding. Laurasia (present-day Europe and North America) smashed into Gondwanaland (present-day Africa and South America) and produced the Appalachian mountain belt. In North America the environment was heavily maritime with seas covering large parts of the continents.

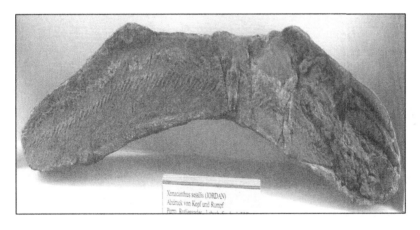

Impression of the head and body of Xenacanthus sessilis. Museum für Naturkunde, Berlin.   *CC BY-SA 3.0*

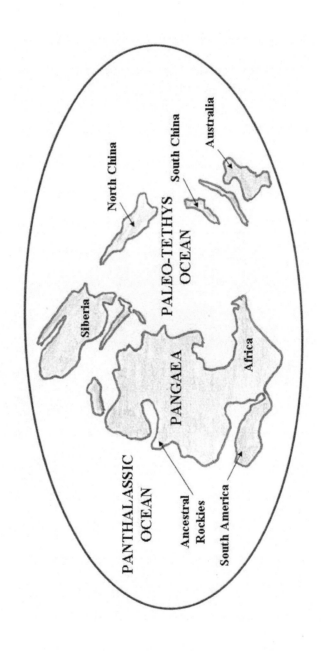

Late Carboniferous (306 Mya)

Permian Period   (290 to 248 Mya)

Eon	Era	Period	Date
Phanerozoic	Paleozoic	Cambrian	540 - 490
		Ordovician	490 - 443
		Silurian	443 - 417
		Devonian	417 - 354
		Carboniferous	354 - 290
		>> Permian	290 – 248

Dielasma
Dimetrodon
Eryops
Glossopteris
Nodosinella

By the beginning of this period, the movement of the plates had brought much of the total land together, fused into the somewhat familiar supercontinent known as **Pangaea**. Most of the continents of today, in *somewhat* intact form, were mashed together and stretched from the northern to the southern poles. Most of the rest of the surface area of the Earth was occupied by a corresponding single ocean, known as Panthalassic Ocean, with a smaller sea to the east of Pangaea known as Tethys Ocean.

It is speculated that the interior regions of this massive continent were probably dry with enormous seasonal fluctuations. Little is known about the oceans themselves at that time, but there are indications that the climate of the Earth shifted, and that glaciations decreased as the interiors of continents became drier.

Because of the aridity, the swamp forests of the Carboniferous were gradually replaced by conifers, seed ferns, and other drought-resistant plants.

Early reptiles were in a good position for this new climate; thick, moisture-retaining skin allowed them to move in where amphibians had previously been dominant. They became ideally suited to the desert-type habitats in which they still thrive today. *Therapsids* found an internal solution to keeping warm; they became warm-blooded, conserving heat generated through the breakdown of food. These more metabolically active reptiles could survive the harsh interior regions and they became the dominant land animals of the late Permian, rapidly evolving many different forms, ranging from dinosaur-like fanged flesh-eaters to plodding herbivores.

In the latter part of the Permian smaller varieties emerged, likely warm-blooded and covered in insulating hair. From them, mammals would arise.

The Permian, and the entire Paleozoic, came to a calamitous close, marking a biological dividing line in the Earth's history that few animals were alive to cross. This extinction is estimated to have extinguished more than 90% of all marine species and 70% of land animals. There are several theories as to the cause of this, ranging from a series of cataclysmic volcanic eruptions to global climate change that the life forms could not adapt, a release of methane gas from beneath the sea and asteroid impact.

Perhaps a combination of factors was to blame. But whatever it was it paved the way for new animals and plants to evolve into the void left by all the lost species. The great forests of fern-like plants shifted to gymnosperms, plants with their offspring enclosed within seeds and to the dinosaurs.

Dimetrodon incisivum, Sphenacodontidae; Permian, Texas, USA;
Staatliches Museum für Naturkunde Karlsruhe, Germany
CC BY-SA 3.0

130

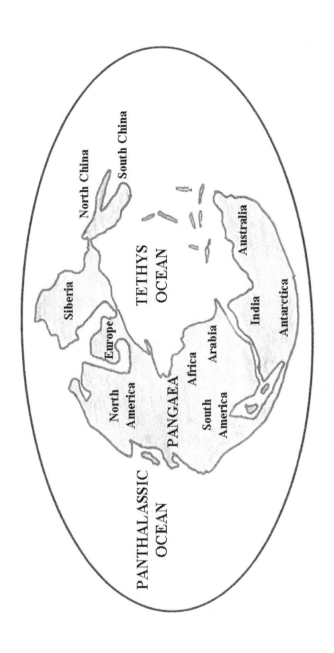

Permian (299 - 248 Mya)

Triassic Period   (248 to 206 Mya)

Eon	Era	Period	Date
Phanerozoic	Mesozoic	>> Triassic	248 - 201
		Jurassic	201 - 145
		Cretaceous	145 - 66

Dictophyllum
Kannemey
Menotiseria
Morganucodon
Pteronisculus

This period marks the end of the largest extinction event in the history of life, and is the part of the story where the surviving species regrouped and re-established themselves in new landscape of the Triassic.

Pangaea began to break apart in the mid-Triassic, forming Gondwana (South America, Africa, India, Antarctica, and Australia) in the south and Laurasia (North America and Eurasia) in the north. The continents were well above sea level, and the sea level did not change drastically during the period. Due to this relationship, flooding of the continents to form shallow seas did not occur. Much of the inland area was isolated from the cooling and moist effects of the ocean. The result was a globally arid and dry climate though regions near the coast most likely experienced seasonal monsoons.

The ocean hosted reptiles such as the dolphin-shaped *ichthyosaurs* and the long-necked and paddle-finned *plesiosaurs* preyed on fish and ancient squid.

The bottom rung of the food chain was filled with microscopic plants called *phytoplankton* first appeared.

Animal life diversified and exploded into a wide variety of creatures. Frogs, salamanders, crocodiles, turtles, and snakes emerged. *Pterosaurs*, a group of flying reptiles, appeared in the skies. On land moss, liverwort, and ferns carpeted the floors of forests of conifers, ginkgoes, and palm-like cycads. Spiders, scorpions, millipedes and centipedes thrived, and grasshoppers appeared for the first time.

But perhaps the biggest changes came with the evolution of *dinosaurs* and the first mammals in the late Triassic. Another extinction event at the end of the Triassic took out a large number of these new life forms, but the dinosaurs survived, and moved into the most well-known period in Earth's history besides the one we occupy now.

Life restoration of Morganucodon watsoni by Nobu Tamura CC BY-SA 4.0

Early Triassic (237 Mya)

Jurassic Period   (201 to 145 Mya)

Eon	Era	Period	Date
Phanerozoic	Mesozoic	>> Jurassic	201 - 145
		Cretaceous	145 - 66

Androdemus
Archaeopteryx
Arnioceras
Cuspiteuthis
Gryphaea
Macroplata
Rhamphorhynchus
Stegosaurus
Williamsonia

The **Jurassic** is a geologic period and stratigraphic system that spanned from the end of the Triassic to the beginning of the Cretaceous. The Jurassic constitutes the middle period of the Mesozoic and is named after the Jura Mountains, where limestone strata from the period were first identified.

The start of the Jurassic was marked by the major Triassic–Jurassic extinction event, associated with the eruption of the Central Atlantic Magmatic Province. The beginning of the Toarcian started around 183 million years ago, and is marked by an extinction event associated with widespread oceanic anoxia, ocean acidification, and elevated the temperatures likely caused by the eruption of the Karoo-Ferrar large igneous provinces. The end of the Jurassic, however, has no clear boundary with the Cretaceous and is the only boundary between geological periods to remain formally undefined.

By the beginning of the Jurassic, the supercontinent Pangaea had begun rifting into two landmasses: Laurasia to the north and Gondwana to the south. The climate of the Jurassic was warmer than the present, and there were no ice caps. Forests grew close to the poles, with large arid expanses in the lower latitudes.

On land, the fauna transitioned from the Triassic fauna, dominated jointly by *dinosauromorph* and *pseudosuchian* archosaurs, to that dominated by dinosaurs alone.

The first birds appeared during the Jurassic, evolving from a branch of *theropod* dinosaurs. Other major events include the appearance of the earliest lizards and the evolution of therian mammals. Crocodylomorphs made the transition from a terrestrial to an aquatic life.

The oceans were inhabited by marine reptiles such as ichthyosaurs and plesiosaurs, while pterosaurs were the dominant flying vertebrates.

Stegosaurus currently exposed at the Houston Museum of Natural Science

Fossil specimen of Rhamphorhynchus munsteri Musée de sciences naturelles de Bruxelles Picture by M0tty CC BY-SA 3.0

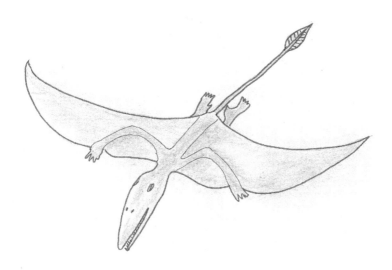

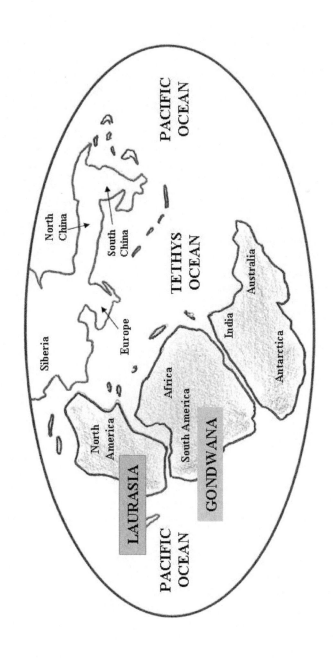

Early Jurassic (201-145 Mya)

Eon	Era	Period	Date
Phanerozoic	Mesozoic	>> Cretaceous	145 - 66

Ginkgo
Globigerma
Hamiles
Hesperornis
Laosciadia
Micraster
Sellithyris
Triceratops

The Cretaceous was a period with a relatively warm climate, resulting in high euxinic sea levels that created numerous shallow inland seas. These oceans and seas were populated with now-extinct marine reptiles, ammonites, and rudists, while dinosaurs continued to dominate on land. The world was ice free, and forests extended to the poles. During this time, new groups of mammals and birds appeared. During the Early Cretaceous, flowering plants appeared and began to rapidly diversify, becoming the dominant group of plants across the Earth by the end of the Cretaceous, coincident with the decline and extinction of previously widespread gymnosperm groups.

The Cretaceous, along with the Mesozoic, ended with the **Cretaceous–Paleogene** extinction event, a large mass extinction in which many groups, including non-avian dinosaurs, pterosaurs, and large marine reptiles, died out. The end of the Cretaceous is defined by the abrupt Cretaceous–Paleogene boundary (K/Pg boundary), a geologic signature associated with the mass extinction that lies between the Mesozoic and Cenozoic eras.

Triceratops mounted skeleton at Los Angeles Museum of Natural History, Los Angeles, USA   CC BY-SA 3.0

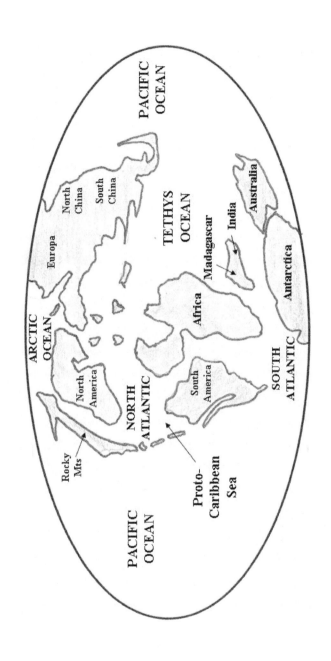

Cretaceous (145 - 66 Mya)

Palaeogene Period   (66 to 25 Mya)

Eon	Era	Period	Date
Phanerozoic	Cenozoic	>> Paleogene	66 - 25
		Neogene	25 - 1.8
		Quarternary	1.8 - Now

Brontotherium
Cornulina
Hipparion
Hyaenodon
Nepa
Sapindus

Paleogene is the beginning of the Cenozoic era of the present Phanerozoic eon. The earlier term Tertiary period was used to define the span of time now covered by the Paleogene and subsequent Neogene Periods. The Paleogene is most notable for being the time during which mammals diversified from relatively small, simple forms into a large group of diverse animals in the wake of the Cretaceous–Paleogene extinction event that ended the preceding Cretaceous period.

This period consists of the Palaeocene, Eocene, and Oligocene epochs. The end of the Palaeocene was marked by the **Palaeocene–Eocene Thermal Maximum**, one of the most significant periods of global change during the Cenozoic, which upset oceanic and atmospheric circulation and led to the extinction of numerous deep-sea benthic foraminifera and on land, a major turnover in mammals. The term **'Paleogene System'** is applied to the rocks deposited during the **'Paleogene Period'**.

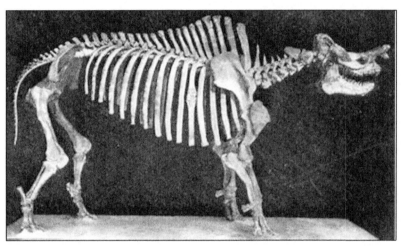

Skeleton of Brontotherium
American Museum of Natural History, New York

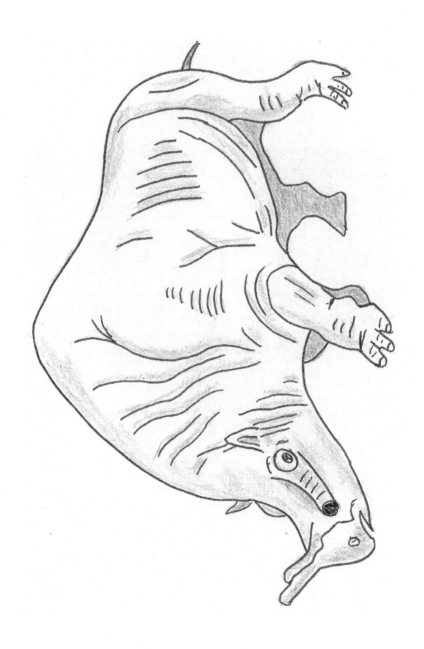

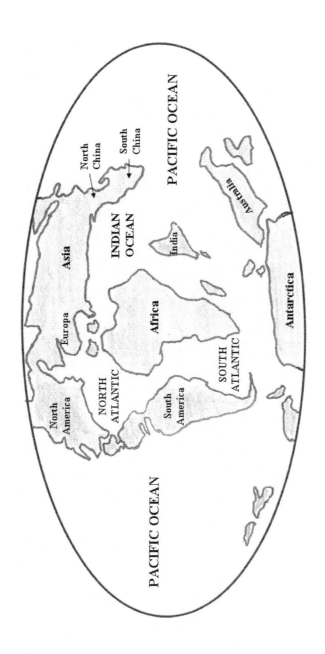

Paleogene (66 - 25 Mya)

145

Selection of Prehistoric Animals across Timeline

Cambrian   543 - 490 mya

          Anomalocaris
          Haikouichthys
          Trilobites

Ordovician   490 - 443 mya

          Cameroceras
          Megalograptus

Silurian   443 - 417 mya

          Brontoscorpio
          Cephalaspis
          Pterygotus

Devonian   417 - 354 mya

          Dunkleosteus
          Hyneria
          Hynerpeton
          Stethacanthus

Carboniferous   354 - 290 mya

          Arthropleura
          Meganeura
          Petrolacosaurus
          Proterogyrinus

Permian   290 - 248 mya

          Diictodon
          Dimetrodon
          Edaphosaurus
          Gorgonops
          Scutosaurus
          Seymouria

Triassic   248 - 206 mya

          Coelophysis
          Cymbospondylus
          Euparkeria
          Lystrosaurus
          Nothosaurus
          Peteinosaurus
          Placerias
          Plateosaurus
          Postosuchus
          Proterosuchus
          Tanystropheus
          Thrinaxodon

Jurassic	206 - 144 mya	Allosaurus
		Ammonites
		Anurognathus
		Brachiosaurus
		Cryptoclidus
		Diplodocus
		Eustreptospondylus
		Hybodus
		Leedsichthys
		Liopleurodon
		Metriorhynchus
		Ophthalmosaurus
		Ornitholestes
		Othnielia
		Rhamphorhynchus
		Stegosaurus
Cretaceous	144 - 65 mya	Anatotitan
		Ankylosaurus
		Archelon
		Argentinosaurus
		Didelphodon
		Elasmosaurus
		Giganotosaurus
		Hesperornis
		Iberomesornis
		Iguanodon
		Koolasuchus
		Leaellynasaura
		Mononykus
		Ornithocheirus
		Polacanthus
		Protoceratops
		Pteranodon
		Sarcosuchus
		Tapejara
		Tarbosaurus
		Therizinosaurus
		Torosaurus
		Tylosaurus
		Tyrannosaurus
		Utahraptor
		Velociraptor
		Xiphactinus
Paleocene	65 - 55 mya	Gastornis

147

Eocene	55 - 34 mya	Ambulocetus
		Andrewsarchus
		Apidium
		Arsinoitherium
		Basilosaurus
		Dorudon
		Embolotherium
		Godinotia
		Leptictidium
		Moeritherium
		Propalaeotherium
Oligocene	34 - 24 mya	Hyaenodon
		Entelodon
		Indricotherium
		Cynodictis
Miocene	24 - 5 mya	Chalicotherium
		Deinotherium
Pliocene	5 - 1.8 mya	Ancylotherium
		Australopithecus afarensis
		Carcharodon megalodon
		Dinofelis
		Doedicurus
		Macrauchenia
		Megatherium
		Odobenocetops
		Phorusrhacos
		Smilodon
Pleistocene	1.8 mya - 10,000 ya	Coelodonta
		Mammuthus
		Megaloceros
		Panthera leo
		Homo floresiensis
		Homo neanderthalensis
		Homo sapiens

Evolution of Earth's Atmosphere

The atmosphere of the Earth has been changing continuously since its formation. The Sun, the Earth and other planets were formed when matter coalesced from a rotating nebula approximately 4,567 million years ago, according to the most widely accepted theory.

The solar nebula originated from the explosion of older stars containing heavy elements like iron that had been created by nuclear fusion of lighter atoms. The accumulation of mass at the centre of the rotating nebula was so large that gravitational compression initiated the fusion of hydrogen into helium thus giving birth to the Sun which became a new shining star. (*refer back to page 29*)

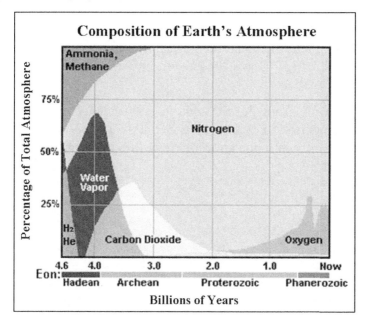

149

The planets orbiting the Sun formed by accretion, the heavier elements concentrated in the cores and the lighter gaseous elements became the atmospheres.

Chemical elements in the Sun include:

hydrogen	(H)	73.46%
helium	(He)	24.85%
oxygen	(O)	0.77%
carbon	(C)	0.29%
iron	(Fe)	0.16%

… and smaller percentages of neon, silicon, magnesium, sulphur etc.

This composition indicates that the nebula from which our solar system originated was mostly hydrogen, helium and small amounts of heavier elements. Planets like Mercury, Venus, Earth and Mars which are close to the Sun lost their hydrogen and helium rapidly because their gravitational pull was not strong enough to retain these light elements (*refer to page 173 on Escape Velicities*).

The loss of hydrogen and helium had the effect of increasing the concentration of heavier gases in the atmospheres of these terrestrial planets.

Further away from the Sun where it is much colder, methane could condense as a liquid, and Saturn's moon Titan has a predominantly nitrogen atmosphere with pools of liquid methane on its surface.

Hadean Eon (4.56 to 4.0 Ga)

When the material forming the Earth coalesced and melted, it organized itself into layers with dense materials at the core and less dense compounds closer to the surface. The gases comprising the atmosphere formed the outermost layer and had a composition similar to that of the gases of the condensing planetary nebula.

During the Hadean, the Earth's surface consisted of molten rock, a magma ocean, and water existed only as steam in the atmosphere.

It is hypothesised that around 4.45 Ga, the Earth experienced a violent collision with a planetoid called **Theia** that was about the size of Mars. It is theorized that this collision added extra mass to the Earth, but a portion of the impact debris went into orbit and accreted to form the Moon.

(In Greek mythology, Theia was the name of a Titaness who was the mother of Selene, the goddess of the Moon, which parallels the planetoid Theia's collision with the early Earth).

Some scientists have proposed that this giant impact blasted away into space the Earth's entire atmosphere, including much of the water, and that the atmosphere and water were subsequently replenished by volcanic out gassing and impacts from asteroids and comets.

A problem with this proposal is that the ratio of deuterium to hydrogen (D/H) for comets is very different from what is found in the Earth's oceans, so comets are not a likely source for Earth's water. Also, volcanic emissions do not have much nitrogen, so it is unlikely that volcanism provided the nitrogen in our current atmosphere. While it is true that a great collision would have sent much of the atmosphere into space, most of it would have remained within the Earth's gravitational sphere of influence and could have been recaptured by the Earth as the debris from the giant impact cooled and was partitioned between the Earth and the newly formed Moon giving both a similar chemical composition.

After the hydrogen and helium had escaped, Earth's Hadean atmosphere was left with methane, ammonia, water vapour, and small percentages of nitrogen and carbon dioxide. A cataclysmic meteorite bombardment around 3.9 Ga kept much of the Earth's surface in the molten state, and the incoming impactors may have brought additional water, methane, ammonia, hydrogen sulphide and other gases that supplemented the atmosphere.

The high surface temperature of the Earth during the Hadean favoured the depletion of atmospheric methane through the endothermic reaction of methane with the steam in the atmosphere. Reactions such as this require high temperatures of approximately 800°C to 1100°C which would have been common in the hot crust and magma lakes of the Hadean Earth.

The resulting carbon monoxide would readily combine with metals to form carbonyl compounds.

$$CH_4 + H_2O^{steam} \rightarrow CO + 3H_2$$

The Hadean was too hot for liquid water to condense on the surface of the Earth, but water vapour would have been able to condense at high altitude in the atmosphere and produce rain that evaporated quickly as it fell when it approached the ground.

Towards the end of the Hadean, volcanic activity started increasing the percentage of carbon dioxide in the atmosphere.

The Earth's surface changed from molten lava to solid rock, and liquid water started to accumulate on the surface.

Archean Eon (4.0 to 2.5 Ga)

The crust of the Earth started to cool down during the Archean. The amount of water vapour in the atmosphere decreased as water started condensing in liquid form. Continuous rainfall for millions of years led to the build-up of the oceans. As steam condensed into water, the atmospheric pressure of the Earth became lower, and the water started dissolving gases like ammonia and removed them from the atmosphere creating ammonium compounds, amines and other nitrogen-containing substances suitable for the origin of life.

$$NH_3 + H_2O \rightarrow NH_4^+ + OH$$

The condensation of water with gases such as sulphur dioxide produced acid rain that created new minerals on the Earth's surface. Volcanic carbon dioxide peaked during the Archean and started to decrease through the formation of carbonate minerals that resulted from reactions of metals with the carbonic acid generated from carbon dioxide and water.

$$CO_2 + H_2O \rightarrow H_2CO_3$$
carbonic acid

Microfossils of **sulphur-metabolizing cells** have been found in 3.4-billion-year-old rocks, and it is known that the first aquatic photosynthetic organisms originated around 3.5 Ga. The oxygen produced by *cyano-bacteria* (*blue-green algae*) during the Archean reacted with the metal ions in the **anoxic** sea.

Billions of years would pass before the photosynthetic micro-organisms could eventually change the composition of the atmosphere.

By the middle of the Archean, the Earth had cooled enough so that most of the water vapour in the atmosphere had condensed as water, and the Earth had its first days without clouds.

At that time the atmosphere comprised:

carbon dioxide	(CO_2)	15%
methane	(CH_4)	only minimal levels
ammonia	(NH_3)	only minimal levels
nitrogen	(N)	75%
oxygen	(O)	negligible

In essence, most of the original components of the atmosphere had escaped, precipitated as liquids or reacted chemically to form solid compounds. The volcanic activity and the photosynthetic bacteria had become the major factors influencing the Earth's atmospheric composition.

The scene had now been set for the greatest show on Earth, the ability for amino acids to be produced from the basic gases now present in the atmosphere.

Carbon dioxide began to be taken up in the water 'sink' which was now forming over wide expanses of the newly formed seas. But more water was to be produced, not necessarily from the bombardment of meteoroids from outer space, or the volcanic rocks, but from the basic components which had now been formed.

As Miller and Urey demonstrated in their epic experiment of 1962, this was not only feasible, but possible.

(refer to back page 96 in Chapter 9 – Geological Eons)

Artist's impression of the Archean Eon. *Tim Bertelink*
CC BY-SA-4.0

Proterozoic Eon (2.5 to 0.54 Ga)

Unicellular life proliferated during the Proterozoic. Anaerobic microbial life thrived in a planet with little oxygen. Anaerobic organisms obtained their energy in various ways. Methanogens combined hydrogen and carbon dioxide to produce methane and water:

$$CO_2 + 4H_2 \longrightarrow CH_4 + 2H_2O$$

Sulphate reducing bacteria combined methane to produce sulphate radicals:

$$CH_4 + SO_4^{--} \longrightarrow HCO_3^- + HS^{\cdot-} + H_2O$$

Other organisms capable of photosynthesis used the energy of sunlight to convert the abundant carbon dioxide and water into carbohydrates and oxygen, which gas was deadly to the anaerobes.

$$6CO_2 + 6H_2O \longrightarrow C_6H_{12}O_6 + 6O_2$$
$$\text{carbohydrate}$$

By the first quarter of the Proterozoic, the Sun had become brighter and its luminosity had increased to 85% of the present level. By this time, most of the carbon dioxide had been depleted from the atmosphere, leaving nitrogen as the main atmospheric gas with a small percentage of oxygen.

Nitrogen gas (N_2), which is quite chemically inert, had been a small percentage of the Earth's atmosphere during the Hadean, but it became the major component of the atmosphere during the Proterozoic once all the other gases were gone.

The Earth's surface and seas contained great quantities of iron that readily combined with oxygen to produce iron oxides. From the beginning of the Proterozoic to 1.85 Ga, atmospheric oxygen levels rose as the rate of photosynthesis increased considerably. Shallow seas became partially oxygenated but the deep oceans continued to be anoxic.

Although photosynthetic organisms had been releasing oxygen since Archean times, the oxygen levels could not build up in the atmosphere because the oxygen was being depleted by the oxidation of metals and by the oxidation of methane to yield carbon dioxide and water in the presence of ultraviolet (UV) radiation.

$$4Fe + 3O_2 \longrightarrow 2Fe_2O_3$$
Oxidation of metallic iron to form iron (III) oxide

$$CH_4 + 2O_2 \longrightarrow CO_2 + 2H_2O$$
Oxidation of methane

The cooling of the Earth during the Proterozoic stabilized the land masses and reduced the volcanic out gassing of carbon dioxide. Methane and carbon dioxide are Greenhouse Gases; their decrease in the atmosphere may have contributed to the **'Huronian glaciation'** that lasted from 2.4 Ga to 2.1 Ga.

The cold temperature sequestered additional methane from the atmosphere by forming **methane clathrate,** a crystal structure of water similar to ice that traps a large amount of methane. An increased period of oxygen production occurred between 2.4 Ga and 2.0 Ga and is known as the **Great Oxidation Event** or **Oxygen Catastrophe**. The higher oxygen level created **banded iron formations (BIF)** by precipitating dissolved iron. The reaction of oxygen with iron in its reduced state (Fe^{2+}) continued to create **BIF** deposits of iron in its oxidized state (Fe^{3+}) until about 1.9 Ga and whenever volcanic activity or crustal plate movements exposed unoxidized iron.

Additional oxygen continued to be consumed by oxidation of minerals on the Earth's crust, but enough free oxygen accumulated in the atmosphere to kill anaerobes near the Earth's surface thus creating an opportunity for the development of aerobic life forms.

Starting around 2.4 Ga, oxygen molecules migrated into the upper atmosphere and formed an **ozone layer**. This is a region in the stratosphere located between 15 to 35 kilometres above the Earth's surface where oxygen molecules (O_2) are converted to ozone (O_3) by the Sun's ultraviolet rays. The reverse conversion of ozone back to oxygen releases heat. The ozone layer basically absorbs high-energy ultraviolet radiation and converts it to heat. The high energy UV light is dangerous for life because it can cause mutations in DNA sequences.

The atmospheric composition was very steady between 1.85 Ga to 0.85 Ga. During this time, Earth's atmosphere had approximately 10% oxygen. Photosynthetic organisms were still producing oxygen at a high rate, but the reaction of oxygen with dissolved minerals in the deep oceans and with rock and clay on the Earth's surface did not allow atmospheric oxygen levels to increase.

By 0.85 Ga, the minerals in the sea and on land could not bind as much oxygen, and the excess oxygen began to accumulate in the atmosphere. With the increased oxygen levels and the protection of the ozone layer, organisms capable of aerobic respiration could now proliferate all over the surface of the Earth.

Phanerozoic Eon (0.542 Ga to present)

The beginning of the Phanerozoic, the Cambrian, is marked by an abundance of multicellular life. Most of the major groups of animals first appeared at this time. Vegetation covered the surface of the Earth, and oxygen accounted for 30% of the atmosphere. Air enriched with so much oxygen allowed giant insects to develop and caused frequent forest fires set off by lightning.

A great mass-extinction event occurred 251 million years ago (0.251 Ga) marking the boundary of the Permian and Triassic. Oxygen levels dropped from 30% to 12%, and carbon dioxide levels reached about 2000 ppm. This was Earth's worst mass extinction and it eliminated 90% of ocean dwellers and 70% of land plants and animals. The cause of this mass extinction is thought to have been a series of volcanic events in Siberia that lasted for about one million years and released large volumes of carbon dioxide and gases containing sulphur, chlorine and fluorine. By 228 million years ago, oxygen levels had risen to about 15% of the atmosphere, and the first dinosaurs appeared.

Oxygen levels continued to increase, and by the end-Cretaceous, 100 million years ago, oxygen had risen to about 23% of the atmosphere. At this time, dinosaurs were well established and modern mammals and birds began to develop. For the last 100 million years, the percentage of oxygen has fluctuated between 18% and 23% to the present level of about 21% of the atmosphere.

Earth's future atmosphere

Since the beginning of the industrial revolution in the 1750s, humans have been burning coal and petroleum products to provide the energy to power machinery. The combustion of fossil fuels has been generating large quantities of the Greenhouse Gases carbon dioxide (CO_2), methane (CH_4), and nitrous oxide (N_2O).

The concentration of atmospheric carbon dioxide today is approximately 400 parts per million (ppm) and the North Pole's mean annual temperature is -20°C.

When the carbon dioxide concentration was 2,000 ppm 55 million years ago during the **Palaeocene–Eocene Thermal Maximum (PETM)**, the North Pole's temperature averaged 23°C.

It is thought that elevated levels of **Greenhouse Gases** will cause **Global Warming** and influence weather patterns. Many cities bordering the coastal areas will be permanently flooded if the ice deposits in Greenland and Antarctica continue to

Evolution of Oxygen

Before photosynthesis evolved, Earth's atmosphere had no free oxygen (O_2). Photosynthetic prokaryotic organisms that produced O_2 as a waste product lived long before the first build-up of free oxygen in the atmosphere, perhaps as early as 3.5 billion years ago. The oxygen they produced though would have been rapidly removed from the oceans by weathering of reducing minerals, most notably iron. This 'rusting' led to the deposition of iron oxide on the ocean floor, forming banded iron.

Banded Iron Formation at the Fortescue Fall, Western Australia. Graeme Churchard, *Bristol, UK   CC BY 2.0*

Oxygen only began to persist in the atmosphere in small quantities about 50 million years before the start of the **Great Oxygenation Event**. This mass oxygenation of the atmosphere resulted in rapid buildup of free oxygen.

In the *absence of plants*, the rate of oxygen production by photosynthesis was slower in the Precambrian, and the concentrations of O_2 attained were less than 10% of today's and probably fluctuated greatly oxygen may even have disappeared from the atmosphere again around 1.9 billion years ago.

These fluctuations in oxygen concentration had little direct effect on life, with mass extinctions not observed until the appearance of complex high-energy molecule, provided life around the start of the Cambrian, 541 million years ago. This provided life with new opportunities. Since the start of the Cambrian, atmospheric oxygen concentrations have fluctuated between 15% and 35% of atmospheric volume.

The maximum of 35% was reached towards the end of the Carboniferous (about 300 million years ago), a peak which may have contributed to the large size of insects and amphibians at that time.

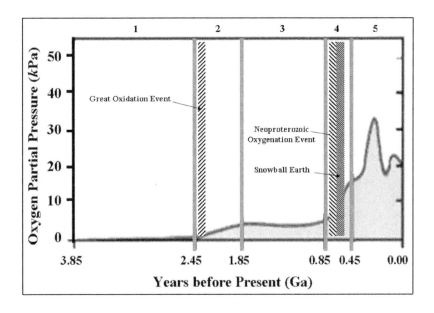

The **Great Oxygenation Event** had the first major effect on the course of evolution. The concentration of oxygen in the atmosphere is often cited as a possible contributor to the **Cambrian explosion** and trends in animal body size.

Biovolume increased dramatically soon after the **Great Oxygenation Event** and this correlates between atmospheric oxygen and maximum body size later in the geological record.

Under low oxygen concentrations and before the evolution of nitrogen fixation, biologically-available nitrogen compounds were in limited supply and periodic 'nitrogen crises' probably rendered the ocean inhospitable to life.

Significant concentrations of oxygen were only one of the prerequisites for the evolution of complex life.

An oxygen-rich atmosphere can release phosphorus and iron from rock, by weathering, and these elements then become available for sustenance of new species whose metabolisms require these elements as oxides.

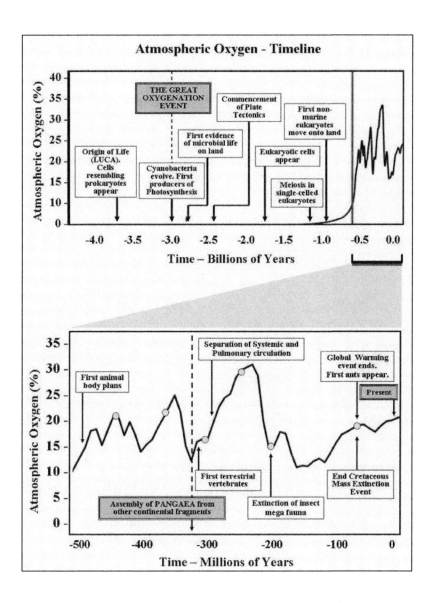

Atmospheric Oxygen - Timeline

Time – Billions of Years

THE GREAT OXYGENATION EVENT

Commencement of Plate Tectonics

First non-marine eukaryotes move onto land

First evidence of microbial life on land

Origin of Life (LUCA). Cells resembling prokaryotes appear

Cyanobacteria evolve. First producers of Photosynthesis

Eukaryotic cells appear

Meiosis in single-celled eukaryotes

Time – Millions of Years

First animal body plans

Separation of Systemic and Pulmonary circulation

Global Warming event ends. First ants appear.

Present

First terrestrial vertebrates

Assembly of PANGAEA from other continental fragments

Extinction of insect mega fauna

End Cretaceous Mass Extinction Event

New study reveals when Earth will run out of Oxygen

Oxygen is an essential element that is commonly accepted as a possible indicator of life on exoplanets. However, the oxygenated atmosphere of Earth that makes it inhabitable may not be permanent.

All oxygen on Earth may disappear in the next one billion years, potentially resulting in the death of all animals and plants on the planet, a new study published in **Nature Geoscience** reveals.

According to the findings, the lifespan of Earth's oxygen-rich atmosphere is estimated to be one billion years. However, the fundamental timescale of the oxygen in our planet's atmosphere remains uncertain.

"For many years, the lifespan of Earth's biosphere has been discussed based on scientific knowledge about the steadily brightening of the sun and global carbonate-silicate geochemical cycle," said researcher Kazumi Ozaki, an assistant professor at Toho University.

The scientists behind the study believe that deoxygenation is 'an inevitable consequence' of increasing solar fluxes, as the Sun is getting older and emitting more heat.

"The atmosphere after the great deoxygenation is characterised by elevated methane, low-levels of CO_2 and no ozone layer. The Earth system will probably be a world of anaerobic life forms," said Ozaki, referring to how creatures that need oxygen to survive will not be able to inhabit the planet.

The findings are based on a model of Earth's atmosphere's evolution that was built with the use of a stochastic approach, allowing the team to carry out a probabilistic assessment of the lifespan of our oxygenated atmosphere.

The model was run over 400,000 times with various parameters to suggest that the oxygen on Earth might only have another billion years to go before solar radiation destroys it.

As the research was conducted as part of NASA's NexSS program that explores the habitability of exoplanets, the team outlined that it might be useful for scientists to consider additional bio signatures applicable to weakly-oxygenated and anoxic worlds in the search for life beyond the solar system.

Daria Bedenko
03:44 GMT 10.03.2021

- **Effects of low oxygen depletion on ecosystem communities and populations:**

OD Level (mg/L)	Qualitative Effect
7 – 15 (19.5%)	Minimum acceptable
5 – 6 (10% - 19.5%)	Impaired judgement
3 – 4 (8% - 10%)	Choking & Nausea
1 – 2 (6% - 8%)	Fatal /Possible recovery
< 1 (4% - 6%)	Coma & Death

- **Effects of low oxygen depletion on chemical composition:**
  - **Converts chemicals to different forms**
    - Carbon dioxide (CO_2) to Methane (CH_4)
    - Sulphate (SO_4) to Hydrogen sulphide (H_2S)
  - **Forms of metals frequently more soluble**
    - Metals can become more mobile
    - Increased exposure of humans and animals to toxic metals

Scientists believe the Earth will eventually run out of Oxygen ... but when?

Climate scientists talk about carbon dioxide a lot. And while it is essential for allowing plants to breathe, it also causes global warming and drastically worsens climate change. Recently, the discussion has shifted to oxygen, the other necessary gas that allows life to flourish on this planet. Apparently, a group of scientists has essentially pinned down **when the Earth will run out of oxygen**, and the results of their analysis might prove somewhat alarming.

Will Earth run out of oxygen?

Yes, sadly, the Earth will eventually run out of oxygen — but not for a *long* time. According to *New Scientist*, oxygen comprises about 21 percent of Earth's atmosphere. That robust concentration allows for large and complex organisms to live and thrive on our planet. The old belief was that oxygen levels during the Mesozoic and Palaeolithic were higher than that and that this was what allowed creatures to grow so large.

Recent theories indicate that those levels may have actually been lower in eons past. The bad news in all that is the prediction that we may eventually see a return to those lower levels sometime in the planet's future.

When will Earth run out of oxygen?

A study published in the journal *Nature Geoscience* and accredited to Kazumi Ozaki and Christopher T. Reinhard explores the future of oxygen on Earth. Through various simulations that modelled climate, biological and geological systems, the study essentially predicted how the conditions might change as years and technologies progressed.

The extrapolated data from these simulations determined that Earth will lose its oxygen-rich atmosphere in approximately **one billion years**. That's the good news. The bad news is that once that happens, the planet will become completely inhospitable for complex aerobic life. Tiny oxygen-breathing critters might survive, as will ones that 'don't technically breathe' like the *tardigrade*, but the rest of us probably won't fare so well.

What is causing oxygen to be depleted?

The shift and eventual loss of oxygen will most likely be caused by the Sun, according to *New Scientist*. As our Sun ages, it becomes hotter, releasing more energy and decreasing the amount of carbon dioxide in the Earth's atmosphere. Without CO_2, plants will not be able to breathe, which means they won't release oxygen into the atmosphere. Ozaki and Reinhard believe that the shift will be rapid, relatively rapid, occurring over the course of 10,000 years... give or take a century.

Andrew Krosofsky
28/4/2021

Hydrogen on Earth

Our planet's hydrogen is mostly locked up in water (H_2O), ammonia (NH_3), hydrogen sulphide (H_2S), methane (CH_4) and other hydrocarbons, and carbohydrates (glucose, fructose etc), as well as within rocks.

Tian et al. (2005) went so far as proposing that a hydrogen-rich atmosphere existed very early in Earth's history. However today, the Earth's atmosphere contains much less than 1 percent hydrogen gas with about 96,500 tonnes of hydrogen being lost to outer space **every year**. That may appear to be a lot, but it is only 1.7×10^{-13} per cent of Earth's supply of molecular hydrogen (H_2) (that is 0.00000000000017%). It would take billions of years to deplete the Earth's vast store of hydrogen.

Gas molecules move freely around in the Earth's atmosphere. Occasionally one of the hydrogen molecules will collide with another one and in doing so transfer energy. If this transferred energy raises the total energy to that greater than the Earth's Escape Velocity of 11.2 (1dp) km/s then the hydrogen molecule can break away from Earth's gravity into outer space and not return.

The kinetic energy of a molecule is:

$$E_k = 0.5 \cdot mv^2$$

If it is assumed that energy is evenly distributed, then it can be seen from the above equation that a molecule with a **lower mass** will have a **greater velocity**. Conversely, a molecule with a greater mass will have a lower velocity. The lighter molecules will therefore have greater velocity and therefore be more likely to attain **Escape Velocity** and leave the Earth's atmosphere.

On Earth, only hydrogen and helium are light enough to attain Escape Velocity in significant numbers.

That is the reason why the composition of the Earth's atmosphere is now mostly comprised of nitrogen, oxygen, and carbon dioxide (CO_2); their kinetic velocity is significantly slower than Earth's Escape Velocity. However, in contrast, when carbon dioxide levels increase or decrease in the atmosphere, the gas does not physically escape Earth. Rather oceans soak up CO_2 like a sponge from biomass photosynthesis.

$$V_{escape} = \sqrt{(2GM / r)}$$

where:

G = Universal Gravitational Constant = 6.67259×10^{-11}
M = Mass of Earth = 5.972×10^{24} kg
r = Radius of Earth = 6,378 km

so:

$$V_{escape} = \sqrt{(2(6.67259 \times 10^{-11} \cdot 5.972 \times 10^{24}))} / 6,378)$$

$$= \mathbf{11.2} \text{ (1dp) km/s}$$

Escape Velocities (km/s)

Sun	617.50
Mercury	4.28
Venus	10.36
Earth	11.18
Mars	5.03

Moon	2.38
Jupiter	60.20
Saturn	36.09
Uranus	21.38
Neptune	23.56

Plate Tectonics and Continental Drift

Plate tectonics is a scientific theory describing the large-scale motion of the plates making up Earth's lithosphere since tectonic processes began on Earth between 3.3 and 3.5 billion years ago. The model builds on the concept of **Continental Drift**, an idea developed during the first decades of the 20th century. The geo-scientific community ultimately accepted plate-tectonic theory after sea-floor spreading was validated in the mid to late 1960s.

Earth's lithosphere is composed of seven or eight major plates and many minor plates. Where the plates meet, their relative motion determines the type of boundary. Earthquakes, volcanic activity, mountain-building, and oceanic trench formation occur along these plate boundaries (or faults). The relative movement of the plates typically ranges from zero to 100 mm annually.

Tectonic plates are composed of the oceanic lithosphere and the thicker continental lithosphere, each topped by its own kind of crust. Along convergent boundaries, the process of *subduction*, or one plate moving under another, carries the edge of the lower one down into the mantle. The area of material lost is roughly balanced by the formation of new (oceanic) crust along divergent margins by seafloor spreading. In this way, the total **geoid** surface area of the lithosphere remains constant.

Tectonic plates are able to move because Earth's lithosphere has greater mechanical strength than the underlying *asthenosphere*. At subduction zones the relatively cold, dense oceanic crust is 'pulled' or sinks down into the mantle over the downward convecting limb of a mantle cell. Another explanation lies in the different forces generated by tidal forces of the Sun and Moon.

This movement leads to what scientists call *'Continental Drift'*. The actual continents move apart and come back together depending on which way the plates on which they are attached are moving. The continents have been all one big landmass at least twice in the history of the Earth when they form **supercontinents**. Tt is surmised that eventually, the continents will come back together again at some point in the future to create a new supercontinent, which is currently dubbed **'Pangaea Ultima'**.

How does continental drift affect evolution? As continents broke apart from Pangaea, species got separated by seas and oceans and speciation occurred. Individuals that were once able to interbreed were isolated from one another, and eventually acquired adaptations that made them incompatible. This drove evolution in creating new species.

Also, as the continents drift, they move into new climates. What was once at the equator may now be near the poles. If species did not adapt to these changes in the weather and temperature, then they would not survive and go extinct. New species would take their place and learn to survive in the new areas.

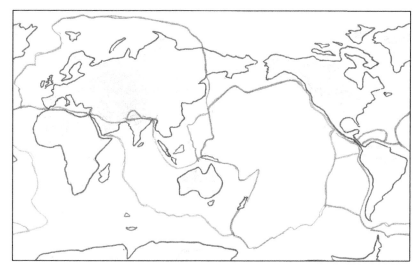

Evolution of Supercontinents

Most commonly, paleogeographers employ the term *supercontinent* to refer to a single landmass consisting of all the modern continents. The earliest known supercontinent was Vaalbara. It formed from proto-continents and was a supercontinent by 3.6 billion years ago (3.6 Ga). **Vaalbara** broke up ~2.8 Ga. The supercontinent Kenorland was formed ~2.5 Ga and then broke sometime after 2.5 Ga into the proto-continent cratons called **Laurentia**, **Baltica**, **Australia** and **Kalahari**.

The supercontinent **Columbia** formed and broke up during a period of 1.8 to 1.5 billion years (1.8-1.5 Ga) ago. The supercontinent, **Rodinia**, broke up roughly 750 million years ago. One of the fragments included large parts of the continents now located in the southern hemisphere. Plate tectonics brought the fragments of **Rodinia** back together in a different configuration during the late Paleozoic, forming the best-known supercontinent, **Pangaea**. **Pangaea** subsequently broke up into the northern and southern supercontinents, **Laurasia** and **Gondwana**.

Modern studies have suggested that supercontinents form in cycles, coming together and breaking apart again, through plate tectonics, very roughly about every 250 million years.

Supercontinents block the flow of heat from Earth's interior, and thus cause the asthenosphere to overheat. Eventually, the lithosphere will begin to dome upward and crack, magma will then rise, and the fragments will be pushed apart.

It is currently a matter of some debate as to how the supercontinents reform, whether or not plate tectonics makes them re-join after travelling around the planet, or if they move apart and then back together again remains, at best, a matter of conjecture.

Throughout Earth's history, there have been many supercontinents. In order of age (oldest to newest), the ancient supercontinents were:

Ancient Supercontinents

Supercontinent Name	Age (Mya)	Period/Era Range
Yilgarn Craton (*)	3,600–2,800	Paleoarchean-Neoarchean
Vaalbara	3,600–2,800	Paleoarchean-Neoarchean
Ur	2,803–2,408	Mesoarchean-Siderian
Kenorland	2,720–2,114	Neoarchean-Rhyacian
Arctica (*)	2,114–1,995	Rhyacian-Orosirian
Atlantica (*)	1,991–1,124	Orosirian-Stenian
Nena (*)	1,900–1,600	Orosirian-Statherian
Columbia (Nuna)	1,820–1,350	Orosirian-Ectasian
Rodinia	1,130–750	Stenian-Tonian
Pannotia (Vendian)	633–573	Ediacaran
Laurasia	550–200	Ediacaran-Triassic
Gondwana	550–175	Ediacaran-Jurassic
Pangaea	336–175	Carboniferous-Jurassic

(*) Not generally regarded as a supercontinent - depending on definition

Yilgarn Craton
3,600-2,800 Mya

Perth

Paleoarchean-Neoarchean

Zircon crystal from the Jack Hills of the Narryer Gneiss Terrane, Yilgarn Craton, Western Australia and also 300 km. south point to a continental crust formation.

Evidence is the high Oxygen[18] values of 8.5 and micro-inclusions of SiO_2 in these zircon crystals are consistent with growth from a granitic source supracrustal material, low-temperature interactions and a liquid ocean.

Vaalbara
3,600-2,800 Mya

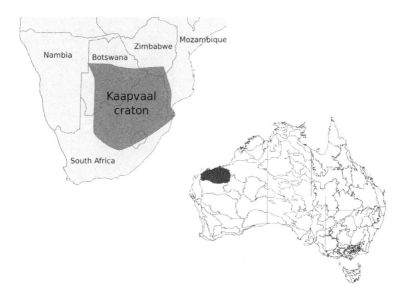

Current locations of Kaapvaal and Pilbara cratons
CC BY-SA 3.0 IBRA 6.1 Pilbara.png

Paleoarchean-Neoarchean

Vaalbara was an Archean supercontinent consisting of the Kaapvaal Craton (now in eastern South Africa) and the Pilbara Craton (now in north-western Western Australia). The name was derived from the last four letters of each craton's name.

The two cratons consist of crust dating from 3.6 to 2.8 Ga, which would make Vaalbara one of Earth's earliest supercontinents.

Ur
2,803-2,408 Mya

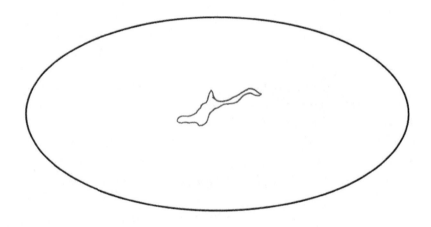

Though probably not a supercontinent, Ur still remains the earliest known continental land mass.

Ur, however, was probably the largest, perhaps even the only continent three billion years ago, so one can argue that Ur was a supercontinent for its time, even if it was smaller than Australia is today. Still an older rock formation has now been located in Greenland and dates back from Hadean.

It is called Ur from the German prefix 'ur' which means 'original', 'fountainhead'. Areas of this supercontinent are now parts of Australia, Africa (Madagascar) and India.

Kenorland
2,700-2,114 Mya

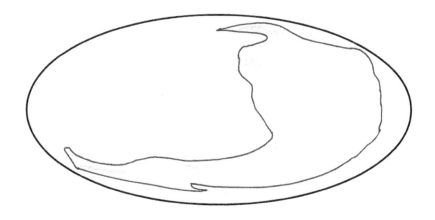

Neoarchean-Rhyacian

Kenorland was one of the earliest known supercontinents on Earth. It is thought to have formed during the Neoarchean by the accretion of Neoarchean cratons and the formation of new continental crust. It comprised what later became Laurentia (the core of today's North America and Greenland), Baltica (today's Scandinavia and Baltic), Western Australia and Kalaharia.

Neoarchean *sanukitoid* cratons and a new continental crust formed Kenorland. Protracted tectonic magna plume rifting occurred between 2.48 to 2.45 Ga and this contributed to the Paleoproterozoic glacial events in 2.45 to 2.22 Ga. Final breakup occurred ~2.1 Ga.

Columbia (aka Nuna)
1,820-1,350 Mya

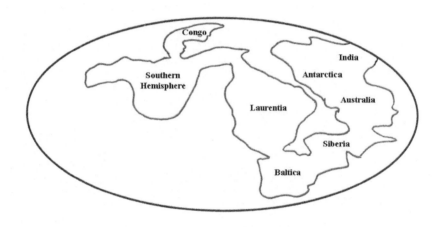

Orosirian-Ectasian

Columbia existed from the beginning of the Statherian until the end of the Calymmian.

It is assumed that the supercontinent was about 4,800 km from North to South and about 12,900 km in its widest part from West to East.

This supercontinent slowly began to break up into parts from 1.6 to 1.2 Ga.

Rodinia
1,130-750 Mya

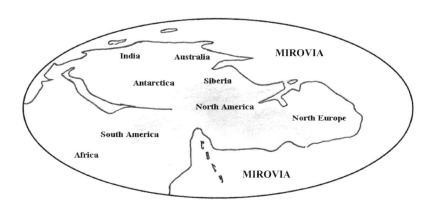

The giant land formation was called **Rodinia** from the Russian 'родина' ('rodina' means 'motherland') or 'родить' ('rodit' means 'to give birth') and the ocean of that time — Mirovia from the Russian 'мир' ('mir' means 'world') or 'мировой' ('mirovoi' means 'worldwide', 'global').

The Earth map was already approaching similarity with its modern version during the existence of Rodinia. By the end of the Tonian the Earth began to turn into a snowball. The theory of '**Snowball Earth**' refers to this period.

Pannotia (aka Vendian)
633-573 Mya

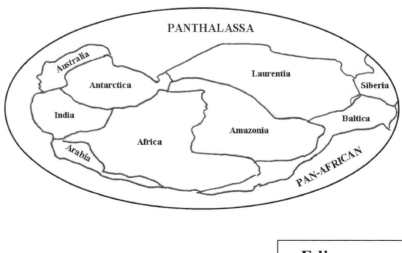

PANTHALASSA

Australia

Antarctica

Laurentia

Siberia

India

Baltica

Amazonia

Africa

Arabia

PAN-AFRICAN

Ediacaran

The formation of **Pannotia** was associated with the break up of Rodinia into Proto-Gondwana and Proto-Laurasia. Since the major part of the land in those days was just near the poles, it is believed that the glaciations reached its peak just about 600 mya.

Also, during the existence of Pannotia there were two proto-oceans - Panthalassa and the Pan-African oceans, which surrounded the supercontinent during the maximum convergence.

At the end of its existence Pannotia broke up into the super continents of Gondwana, Baltica, Siberia and Laurentia.

Laurasia
550-200 Mya

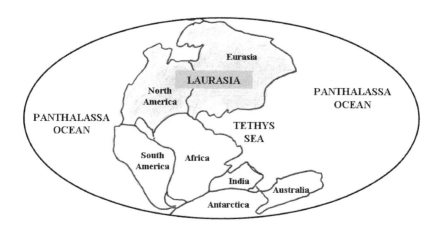

Ordovician Mass Extinction (440 Mya)

Laurasia was the more northern of two large landmasses that formed part of the Pangaea supercontinent, the other being Gondwana. It separated from Gondwana 215 to 175 Mya (beginning in the late Triassic) during the break-up of Pangaea, drifting farther north after the split and finally broke apart with the opening of the North Atlantic Ocean ᶜ56 Mya.

Laurasia finally became an independent continental mass when Pangaea broke up into Gondwana and Laurasia.

Gondwana
550-175 Mya

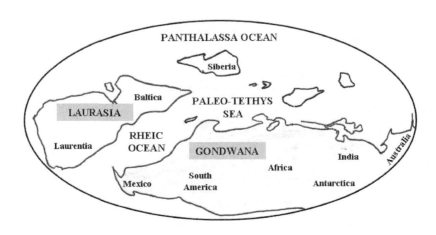

Ordovician Mass Extinction (440 Mya)

Gondwana was a supercontinent that formed during the late Neoproterozoic and began to break up during the Jurassic, with the final stages of break-up, including the opening of the Drake Passage separating South America and Antarctica occurring during the Paleogene.

It was formed by the accretion of several cratons. Eventually, Gondwana became the largest piece of continental crust of the Paleozoic covering an area of about 100,000,000 km^2 about one-fifth of the Earth's surface. During the Carboniferous, it merged with Euramerica to form a larger supercontinent called Pangaea.

South America, India, Australia and Antarctica formed from Gondwana respectively.

Pangaea
336-175 Mya

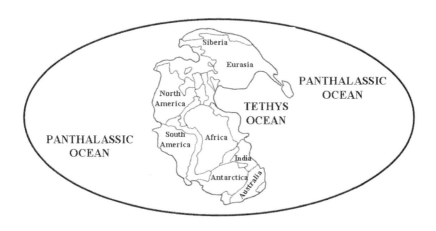

Carboniferous-Jurassic

Permian Mass Extinction (250 Mya)
End Triassic Mass Extinction (200 Mya)

At the time **Pangaea** existed, the super continent united all modern continents into one. Many of today's mountain ranges were formed at the time of collision of continents and lithospheric plates. The outlines of Pangaea are the most accurate since the existence of the super continent is not ancient as that of the previous ones.

At the end of its existence, Pangaea split into Northern and Southern continents - Laurasia and Gondwana. Modern Eurasia and North America formed from Laurasia and Africa. The close-knitted formation of Pangaea gave rise to the movement of various migrant species of fauna as well as flora until the eventual break-up of the supercontinent into separate sub-continents.

Evolution of Supercontinents

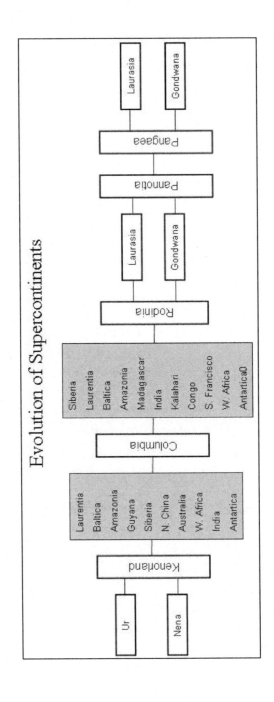

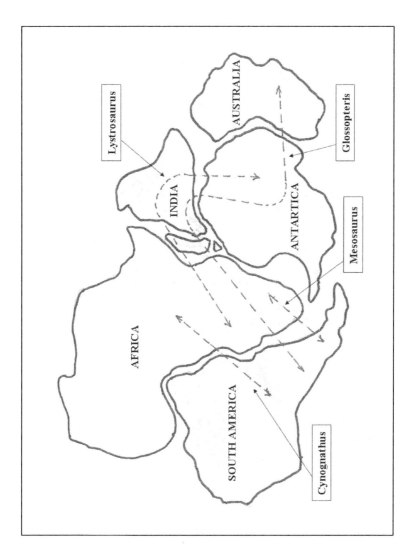

The close-knitted formation of Pangaea gave rise to the movement of various migrant species of fauna as well as flora until the eventual break-up of the supercontinent into separate sub-continents.

187

Impact Events

Evidence of Impact Events (Geological)

- **Spherules**
- **Shocked Quartz**
- **Shatter Cones**
- **Iridium**
- **Rock Dating**

Evidence of Impact Events (Craters)

Impact Craters on the Moon's Surface

Early Impact Craters

Evidence of Impact Events (Geological)

Big impacts can form a thin layer of bits of glass that cover most of the earth's surface. The glass that goes a long way is most likely to have flown in the air as small droplets, known as **spherules**.

The global extent of the Cretaceous–Paleogene (K/Pg) boundary layer proves that **spherules** *generated by one large impact can carpet the surface of the entire planet.*

189

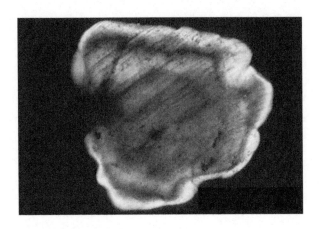

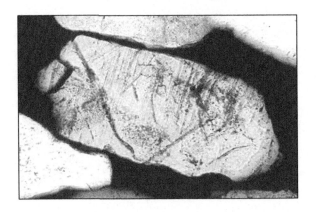

Shocked quartz *is found worldwide, and occurs in the thin* **Cretaceous–Paleogene boundary layer***, which occurs at the contact between Cretaceous and Paleogene rocks. This is further evidence (in addition to iridium enrichment) that the transition between the two geologic periods was caused by a large impact.*

Shatter cones *are distinctive cone or fan-shaped features in rocks, with radiating fracture lines that resemble a horsetail. They are found only in nuclear test sites and* **meteorite** *impact structures. They are formed as a result of the high pressure, high velocity shock wave produced by a large impacting object or a large explosion.*

Iridium is found in meteorites in much higher abundance than in the Earth's crust. For this reason, the unusually high abundance of iridium in the clay layer at the Cretaceous–Paleogene boundary this gave rise to the **Alvarez hypothesis** that the impact of a massive extraterrestrial object caused the extinction of dinosaurs and many other species 66 million years ago.

Impact Craters on the Moon's Surface

Near Side

Far Side

Evidence of Impact Events (Craters)

Early Impact Craters

Name	Country	Location	Diameter (km)	Age (million years) (rounded)	Geological Period
Precambrian					
* Dhala	India	Madhya Pradesh	11	2400 (est)	Paleoproterozoic
* Yarrabubba	Australia	Western Australia	30-80	2229	"
* Vredefort	South Africa	Free State	160	2023	"
Sudbury Basin	Canada	Ontario	130	1849	"
* Shoemaker	Australia	Western Australia	30	1630	Proterozoic
Keurusselkä	Finland	Central Finland	27	1450	Mesoproterozoic
* Strangways	Australia	Northern Territory	24-40	646	Neoproterozoic
Amelia Creek	Australia	Northern Territory	20	630	"
Beaverhead	United States	Idaho and Montana	60	600	"
* Acraman	Australia	South Australia	20	580	Ediacaran
Paleozoic					
Presqu'île	Canada	Quebec	24	500	Cambian
* Clearwater East	Canada	Quebec	23	460-470	Ordovician
Slate Islands	Canada	Ontario	32	450	"
Charlevoix	Canada	Quebec	54	450	"
Siljan Ring	Sweden	Dalarna	52	377	Devonian
Wilkes Land Crater	Antarctica	Wilkes Land	480	375 (?)	"
Woodleigh	Australia	Western Australia	120	364	Carboniferous
Warburton Basin	Australia	Southern Australia	200	360-300	"
Tunnunik	Canada	Northwest Territories	25	360-130	"
Falkland Plateau	Falkland Islands	Offshore	250	300 (?)	Paleozoic
Bedout	Australia	Offshore	250	250	Permian
* Clearwater West	Canada	Quebec	36	290	"
Mesozoic					
* Araguainha	Brazil	Central Brazil	40	255	Permian/Triassic
Triassic	Canada	Manitoba	40	227	Jurassic
Manicouagan	Canada	Quebec	100	214	"
Rochechouart	France	France	23	203-207	"
Puchezh-Katunki	Russia	Nizhny Novgorod	40	195	"
Obolon'	Ukraine	Poltava Oblast	20	169	"
Morokweng	South Africa	Kalahari Desert	75-80	146	"
* Gosses Bluff	Australia	Northern Territory	22	142	Cretaceous
Mjølnir	Norway	Barents Sea	40	142	"
Tookoonooka	Australia	Queensland	55-66	128	"
Steen River	Canada	Alberta	25	91	"
Lappajärvi	Finland	Western Finland	23	78	"
Manson	United States	Iowa	35	74	"
Kara	Russia	Nenetsia	65	70	"
Cenozoic					
* Chicxulub	Mexico	Yucatán	150	66	Cretaceous/Pg
Boltysh	Ukraine	Kirovohrad Oblast	24	65	Paleogene
Shiva Crater	India	Offshore	500	65	"
Montagnais	Canada	Nova Scotia	45	51	"
Kamensk	Russia	S. Federal District	25	49	"
Logancha	Russia	Siberia	20	40	"
Haughton	Canada	Nunavut	23	39	"
Mistastin	Canada	Newfoundland & Labrador	28	36	"
* Popigai	Russia	Siberia	100	36	"
Chesapeake Bay	United States	Virginia	40	35	"
Karakul	Tajikistan	Pamir Mountains	52	20	Neogene
Nördlinger Ries	Germany	Bavaria, Baden	24	14	"
Carswell	Canada	Saskatchewan	39	12	"

194

Chicxulub Crater, Yucatán Peninsula, Mexico

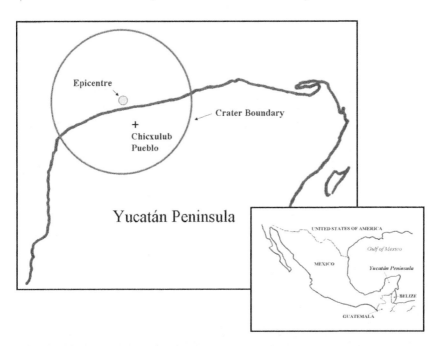

The **Chicxulub impact event** was a ~100 million megaton blast that devastated the Gulf of Mexico region. The blast from the impact generated a core of superheated plasma in excess of 10,000 degrees. Although that thermal pulse would have been relatively short-lived, a handful of minutes, it would have been lethal for nearby life.

The Chicxulub Impact event produced a shock wave and air blast that radiated across the seas, over coastlines, and deep into the continental interior. Winds far in excess of 1,000 km/h were possible near the impact site, although they decreased with distance from the impact site. The pressure pulse and winds would have scoured soils and shredded vegetation and any animals living in nearby ecosystems. An initial estimate of the area damaged by an air blast was in a range of radii from ~900 to ~1,800 km.

That debris landed within minutes in the Gulf of Mexico and Caribbean region. Depending on distance from the impact site, the debris was rocky rubble, impact melted *spherules*, or mixtures of both. Life on the continental landscape and marine seafloor was buried beneath impact *ejecta* that was several hundred metres thick near the impact site and decreased with radial distance.

Since the impact occurred at sea, tsunamis radiated across the Gulf of Mexico, crashing onto nearby coastlines, and also radiated farther across the proto-Caribbean and Atlantic basins. Estimates of the sizes of the waves vary. Lower estimates suggest the waves were only 50 to 100 meters high, while some estimates suggest the *tsunamis* were 100 to 300 meters high when they crashed onto gulf shores and tore through coastal ecosystems. The tsunamis may have penetrated more than 100 kilometres inland before the backwash swept continental debris back into the Gulf of Mexico, where it was deposited in seafloor channels. Both the initial waves and the resulting backwash deeply eroded the seafloor to depths of several hundred metres.

The impact also generated a seismic pulse roughly equivalent to a magnitude 10 earthquake. That seismic activity caused huge landslides on the seafloor, ripping through any colonies of life.

Another classic location is Arroyo el Mimbral in Mexico, where the boundary sediments are several metres thick, and very complex, because of their proximity to the Chicxulub crater. The lower portion of the sequence is composed of altered impact melt *spherules*.

Those global processes were driven by the production of a vapour-rich plume of material that rose from the crater, accelerated through the atmosphere, and expanded around the Earth in space, before raining back down through the atmosphere. The returning cloud of debris carried solid, molten, and vapour products that severely skewed environmental conditions. The environmental health of the Earth would not be the same for a very long time and most life was unable to cope with the changes.

Calculations of impact debris raining from space back through the atmosphere suggests that debris shock-heated the atmosphere, driving chemical reactions that generated nitric acid rain Additional **nitric acid rain** may have also been produced by impact-generated wildfires This acid rain may have fallen over a period of a few months to a few years.

Because the Chicxulub impact occurred in a region with rocks composed of the mineral anhydrite, which is a calcium sulphate mineral, sulphur vapour was also injected into the stratosphere. The sulphur, reacting with water vapour, produced sulphate *aerosols* and eventually **sulphuric acid rain**.

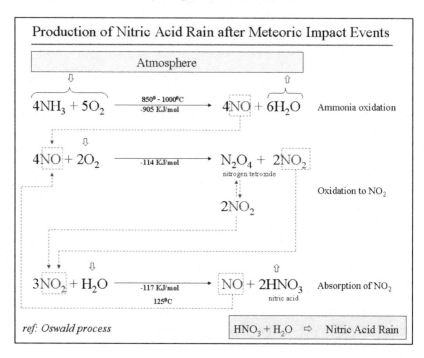

The combination of sulphuric acid rain and nitric acid rain produced by the Chicxulub impact event would have affected vegetation, effectively damaging the base of the continental food web.

Evidence of impact-generated fires was recovered from K-Pg boundary sediments before it was understood how the fires were produced. Several types of carbon indicated fire had swept over some continental regions. In addition to the soot, there is a biological signature that may reflect the recovery of plants in charred regions.

The distribution of those fires is still poorly understood. Although soot is found globally, it is an airborne particulate and, thus, not a good indicator of where fires were ignited. Model calculations have suggested a range of possibilities. The global distribution of iridium indicates *ejecta* was distributed globally, which potentially caused widespread atmospheric heating and fires.

The amount of soot recovered from K-Pg boundary sediments implies the fires released huge amounts of greenhouse gases (carbon dioxide, carbon monoxide, and methane) that likely had a long-term effect on post-impact climate.

Calculations of an atmosphere choked with dust and sulphate *aerosols* from the impact event, and soot from post-impact wildfires, suggest surface temperatures fell and sunlight was unable to reach the Earth's surface, shutting down photosynthesis. A shut-down of photosynthesis may have been the most severe of the impact's environmental effects.

It would have taken a few hours to approximately a year for particles to settle through the atmosphere. The time depended on particle sizes. Relatively large ~250 micron diameter *spherules* found in some K-Pg boundary deposits would have settled out of the atmosphere within hours to days. However, submicron dust may have been suspended in the atmosphere for many months.

Soot, if it was able to rise into the stratosphere, would have taken similarly long times to settle. Soot that only rose into the troposphere, however, would have been promptly flushed out of the atmosphere by rain. The dust, aerosols, and soot may have caused significant decreases in surface temperature of several degrees to a few tens of degrees.

The vaporization of the projectile and a portion of target rocks would have produced ozone-destroying chlorine and bromine. Additional chlorine and bromine were produced when vegetation was burned by post-impact wildfires.

The amounts of those chemicals injected into the atmosphere were far more than that needed to destroy the *ozone layer*. The changes in nitrogen chemistry generated by the atmospheric heating also had the capacity to destroy ozone. The loss of the ozone layer may have lasted for several years, although it is uncertain how much of an effect it had on surface conditions. Initially, dust, soot, and nitrogen molecules in the atmosphere may have absorbed any ultraviolet radiation and sulphate *aerosols* may have scattered the radiation.

Greenhouse gases (carbon dioxide, water, methane) were produced from Chicxulub's target lithologies and the impactor. Those gases may have caused greenhouse warming after the dust, aerosols, and soot settled to the ground. A lot of the carbon dioxide would have come from carbonate rocks on the Yucatán Peninsula. Those rocks, when vaporized, produce carbon dioxide. Water was liberated from the saturated sedimentary sequence and overlying sea.

It would have taken far longer for gases like carbon dioxide to settle out of the atmosphere than dust and sulphate aerosols, so greenhouse warming probably occurred after a period of cooling caused by the dust and aerosols. There are several estimates for the amount of heating, ranging from a global mean average temperature increase of 1 to 1.5°C, based on estimates of CO_2 added to the atmosphere by the impact, to an increase of ~7.5°C, based on measurements of fossilized leaves that grew after the impact event.

(*See also Breaking News at the end of this Chapter*)

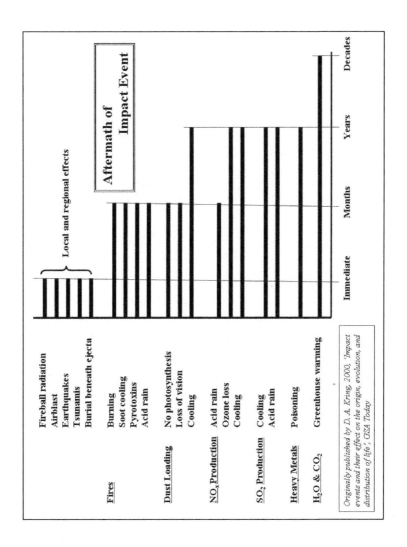

Fires
- Fireball radiation
- Airblast
- Earthquakes
- Tsunamis
- Burial beneath ejecta

Dust Loading
- Burning
- Soot cooling
- Pyrotoxins
- Acid rain

NO$_x$ Production
- No photosynthesis
- Loss of vision
- Cooling

SO$_2$ Production
- Acid rain
- Ozone loss
- Cooling

Heavy Metals
- Cooling
- Acid rain

H$_2$O & CO$_2$
- Poisoning
- Greenhouse warming

Originally published by D. A. Kring, 2000, 'Impact events and their effect on the origin, evolution, and distribution of life', GSA Today

Local and regional effects

Aftermath of Impact Event

Immediate — Months — Years — Decades

Dhala Crater, Madhya Pradesh, India

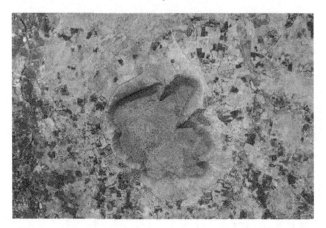

Dhala crater is a crater formed by an asteroid impact. It is situated near Bhonti village in Pichhore block of Shivpuri district of Madhya Pradesh state in India.

It is the largest crater in India, and between the Mediterranean and Southeast Asia. The diameter of the structure is estimated to be 11 km. It is the second such crater found in India, after Lonar Lake.

It is estimated that the impact occurred between 2.44 and 2.24 Ga. Basement rocks are predominantly composed of *granitoids*.

Yarrabubba crater, Western Australia

The **Yarrabubba crater** is an impact structure, the eroded remnant of an impact crater, situated in the northern Yilgarn Craton near Yarrabubba Station between the towns of Sandstone and Meekatharra, Mid West Western Australia.

The rim of the original crater has been completely eroded and is not readily visible on aerial or satellite images. It is centred on a feature called the Barlangi Rock.

The evidence for the extent of impact comes from the presence of *shocked quartz* and *shatter cones* in outcrops of granite interpreted to be near the centre of the original crater, and from geophysical data. The diameter of the original crater is uncertain, but has been estimated to be from 30 to 70 km.

The impact has been dated to 2,229 million years ago, making it the world's oldest **confirmed** impact crater. This date places the impact at the end of the first period when the Earth was mostly or completely frozen, commonly called the **Huronian glaciation**.

The age finding was based on analysis of ancient crystals of the minerals zircon and monazite found in the crater. Scientists used uranium-lead dating to analyze the samples and to determine the age of the impact crater.

Vredefort Crater, Free State, South Africa

The Vredefort crater is **the largest verified impact crater on Earth.** It was 160–300 km across when it was formed; what remains of it is in the present-day Free State province of South Africa. It is named after the town of Vredefort, which is near its centre.

Although the crater itself has long since been eroded away, the remaining geological structures at its centre are known as the Vredefort impact structure. The crater is calculated to be 2,023 million years old, with impact being in the Paleoproterozoic.

The asteroid that hit Vredefort is estimated to have been one of the largest ever to strike Earth (at least since the Hadean some four billion years ago, thought to have been approximately 10–15 km in diameter.

It would have been larger than the Sudbury Basin and the Chicxulub crater. The remaining structure, the Vredefort Dome, consists of a partial ring of hills 70 km in diameter, and is the remains of a dome created by the rebound of rock below the impact site after the collision.

Shoemaker Crater, Western Australia

Formerly known as **Teague Ring** in Western Australia and located around 100 km northeast of the small town Wiluna, the Shoemaker Impact Structure was renamed in honour of Eugene Shoemaker, a planetary geologist and pioneer in impact crater studies.

The almost circular shape of the Shoemaker impact site, visible in the bottom-right of the image, is approximately 30 km in diameter and is defined by concentric rings formed in sedimentary rocks.

The precise age of the impact is unknown, but is estimated to be around 1,630 million years old, making it Australia's oldest impact crater.

Strangways Crater, Northern Territory, Australia

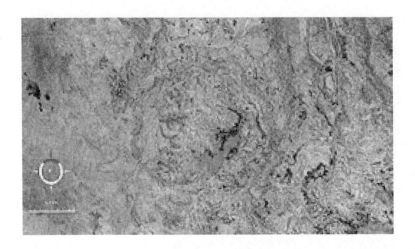

Strangways is a large impact structure, the eroded remnant of a former impact crater, situated in the Northern Territory, Australia. It was named after the nearby Strangways River. The location is remote and difficult to access.

The circular topographic feature that marks the site was originally thought to be volcanic; however an impact origin was first proposed in 1971 after the discovery of evidence of impact including *shatter cones* and *shocked quartz.*

The circular topographic feature is about 16 km in diameter and lies within Neoproterozoic sedimentary rocks of the McArthur Basin.

However, this is only a relic of the original crater after considerable erosion. Estimates of the original rim diameter vary between different researchers in the range 24–40 km.

Acraman Crater, South Australia

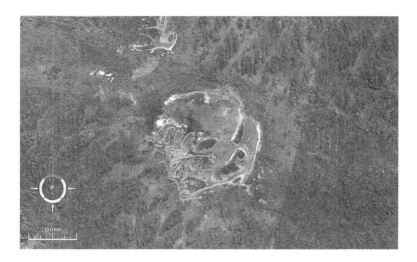

Some 580 million years ago during the Ediacaran, geologists estimate a massive asteroid slammed into what is now South Australia. One remnant of that impact is **Lake Acraman**, a small, shallow salt lake in the arid Australian outback.

The Moderate Resolution Imaging Spectroradiometer (MODIS) on NASA's Terra satellite captured this photo of Lake Acraman and its surroundings on 18th February, 2010. Orange and brown soils mix with off-white saltpans, including Lake Gardiner and Lake Everard in this true-colour image.

Acraman is a complex crater. Rather than the simple bowl shape that is often associated with craters, Acraman has a complicated surface with variations in elevation. Geological studies have found that, over time, Acraman's surface eroded several kilometres below the original crater floor. Studies of the current land surface and debris ejected by the collision suggest that the impact produced an uplifted ring spanning roughly 40 km in the crater's centre.

The rim surrounding the inner ring may have spanned 85 to 90 km, and the total area of disturbed rocks might have been as wide as 150 km.

Radiometric dating of the rocks affected by the Acraman impact indicates that the event occurred around 580 million years ago, during a geologic period known as the Ediacaran. Although our planet was more than 4 billion years old at that time, it was still before the time when life forms began leaving behind a rich fossil record. Nevertheless, fossils do occur in Ediacaran rock layers, and many of them are *acritarchs* - small (often microscopic) fossils that could result from a wide range of organisms.

A dramatic change in the types of *acritarchs* found in the Ediacaran rock record coincides with the estimated occurrence of the Acraman impact.

Although some studies have linked this fossil turnover to a nearly worldwide glaciation, others have suggested the Acraman impact as a possible cause of the widespread disturbance to life on Earth at that time.

Acritarch from the Weng'an biota
c.570–609 Mya

Clearwater Lakes Craters, Baie-d'Hudson, Quebec

The **Clearwater Lakes** occupy the near-circular depressions of two *astroblemes*. The eastern and western craters are 23 km and 36 km in diameter, respectively. Both craters were previously believed to have the same age (290 million years - Permian period), promoting the long-held idea that they formed simultaneously.

Clearwater East and Clearwater West are both complex craters with distinct central peaks. These peaks are caused by the gravitational collapse of crater walls and subsequent rebound of the compressed crater floor. Lake water and sediments cover the central peak of Clearwater East, but bathymetric surveys of the lake floor and core drilling confirm the presence of a peak in its centre.

Dating of impact melt rocks from both impact craters suggests that **Clearwater East** has an age of approximately 460–470 million years, corresponding to the Middle Ordovician time period.

Clearwater West was formed 290 million years ago, in the Early Permian.

Araguainha Crater, Brazil

The **Araguainha** crater is **an impact crater on the border of Mato Grosso and Goiás states, Brazil between the villages of Araguainha and Ponte Branca.** With a diameter of 40 km, it is the largest known impact crater in South America.

The crater has most recently been dated to 255 million years ago, when the region was probably a shallow sea. The margins of error of this date overlap the time of the Permian–Triassic extinction event, one of the largest mass extinction events in Earth's history.

The impact punched through Paleozoic sedimentary units belonging to the Paraná Basin formations, and exposed the underlying Ordovician granite basement rocks. It is estimated that the crater was initially 24 km wide and 2.4 km deep, which then widened to 40 km as its walls subsided inwards.

Gosses Bluff, Northern Territory, Australia

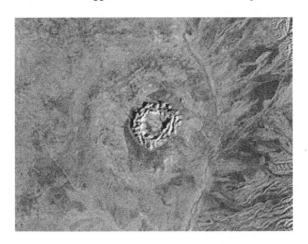

The original crater is thought to have been formed by the impact of an asteroid or comet approximately 142 million years ago,' in the earliest Cretaceous, very close to the Jurassic - Cretaceous boundary.

The original crater rim has been estimated at about 22 km in diameter, but this has been eroded away. The 5 km diameter, 180m high crater-like feature, which is now exposed, is interpreted as the eroded relic of the crater's central uplift.

The impact origin of this topographic feature was first proposed in the 1960s, the strongest evidence coming from the abundance of *shatter cones*.

Popigai Crater, Siberia, Russia

The **Popigai** crater in Siberia, Russia, is tied with the Manicouagan Crater as the fourth largest verified impact crater on Earth. A large *bolide* meteor impact created the 100 kilometre diameter crater approximately 36 million years ago during the Paleogene.

It might be linked to the Eocene–Oligocene extinction event. The crater is 300 km east from the outpost of Khatanga and 880 km northeast of the city of Norilsk. It is designated by UNESCO as a Geopark, a site of special geological heritage. There is a small possibility that the Popigai impact crater may have formed simultaneously with the approximately 35-million-year-old Chesapeake Bay and Toms Canyon impact craters. For decades the Popigai crater has fascinated palaeontologists and geologists, but the entire area was completely off limits because of the diamonds found there.

The shock pressures from the impact instantaneously transformed graphite in the ground into diamonds within a 13.6 km radius of the impact point.

*The **Huronian glaciation** (or **Makganyene glaciation**) was a glaciation that extended from 2.4- 2.1 billion years ago, during the Siderian and Rhyacian periods of the Paleoproterozoic.*

*The Huronian glaciation followed the **Great Oxygenation Event,** a time when increased atmospheric oxygen decreased atmospheric methane. The oxygen combined with the methane to form carbon dioxide and water, which do not retain heat as well as methane does. The glaciation led to a mass extinction on Earth.*

Breaking News

More than one asteroid could have spelled doom for the dinosaurs

A newly discovered impact crater spanning more than 5 miles, the Nadir crater, is buried up to 1,300 feet below the seabed about 250 miles off the coast of Guinea, West Africa.

It hints at the possibility that more than one asteroid hit Earth during the time when dinosaurs went extinct and could force researchers to rethink how the dinosaurs reached the end of their reign.

It is believed that the crater was caused by an asteroid colliding with Earth around 66 million years ago - around the same time that the Chicxulub asteroid hit Earth off the coast of today's Yucatan, Mexico, and wiped out the dinosaurs.

Veronica Bray, a research scientist in the University of Arizona Lunar and Planetary Laboratory, who specializes in craters found throughout the solar system said "This would have generated a tsunami over 3,000 feet high, as well as an earthquake of more than magnitude 6.5 … although it is a lot smaller than the global cataclysm of the Chicxulub impact, Nadir will have contributed significantly to the local devastation".

Phys.org 18 August, 2022

Murchison Meteorite

The **Murchison meteorite** is a meteorite that fell in Australia on 28 September 1969 near Murchison, Victoria.

A bright fireball was observed to separate into three fragments before disappearing, leaving a cloud of smoke. About 30 seconds later, a tremor was heard. Many fragments were found scattered over an area larger than 13km^2 with individual masses up to 7kg. The total collected mass of the meteorite exceeds 100kg.

In January 2020, astronomers reported that particles within the meteorite had been determined to be **7 billion years old**, 2.5 billion years older than the 4.54 billion years age of the Earth and the Solar System, and the oldest material found on Earth to date.

Several lines of evidence indicate that the interior portions of well-preserved fragments from Murchison are pristine. A study using high resolution analytical tools identified no less than 14,000 molecular compounds, including over 70 amino acids, in a sample of the meteorite.

The limited scope of the analysis provided for a potential 50,000 or more unique molecular compositions, with an estimation of the possibility of millions of distinct organic compounds.

What makes Murchison Meteorite special?

It has now been established that the Murchison meteorite contained common amino acids such as *glycine*, *alanine*, and *glutamic acid* as well as unusual ones such as *isovaline* and *pseudoleucine*.

A complex mixture of *alkanes* was also isolated,- similar to that found in the **Miller–Urey experiment**. In fact, the proportions of the amino acids found approximated the proportions proposed to exist in the primitive atmosphere modelled in the original experiment.

A specific family of amino acids called *diamino acids* was also identified. However, significantly, *serine* and *threonine* usually considered to be earthly contaminants were conspicuously absent in all the samples examined.

Measured *purine* and *pyrimidine* compounds were found in the meteorite and strongly indicate a non-terrestrial origin for these compounds. The meteoric specimens demonstrate that many organic compounds could have been delivered by early solar system bodies and may have played a key role in life's origin.

That makes the stardust grains in the meteorite as being 'pre-solar' grains, since they originated at a time **before the Sun was formed**.

Mass Extinctions

What are Mass Extinctions and what caused them?

More than 99% of all organisms that have ever lived on Earth are extinct. As new species evolve to fit ever changing ecological niches, older species fade away. But the rate of extinction is far from constant. At least a number of times in the last 500 million years, 75% to more than 90% of all species on Earth have disappeared in a geological blink of an eye in catastrophes we call **Mass Extinctions**.

Though **mass extinctions** are deadly events, they open up the planet for new forms of life to emerge. The most studied mass extinction, which marked the boundary between the Cretaceous and Paleogene about 66 million years ago, killed off the non-avian dinosaurs and made room for mammals and birds to rapidly diversify and evolve.

Though the **Cretaceous-Paleogene** extinction is notable for being caused mainly by a huge asteroid, it is the exception. The single biggest driver of mass extinctions appears to be major **changes in Earth's carbon cycle** such as large igneous province eruptions, huge volcanoes that flooded hundreds of thousands of square miles with lava. These eruptions ejected massive amounts of heat-trapping gases such as carbon dioxide into the atmosphere, enabling runaway **global warming** and related effects such as ocean acidification and anoxia, a loss of dissolved oxygen in water.

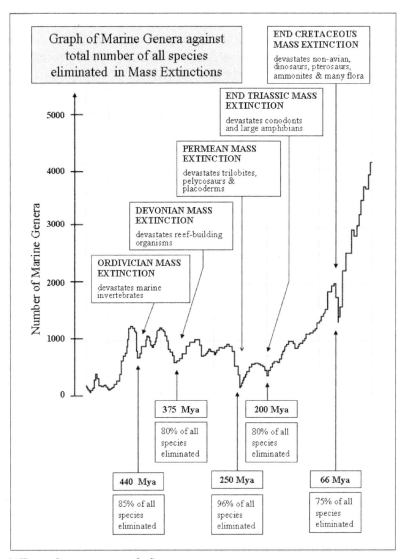

(All numbers are rounded)

Ordovician-Silurian extinction (440 Mya)

The Ordovician was a time of dramatic changes for life on Earth. Over a 30-million-year stretch, species diversity blossomed, but as the period ended, the first known mass extinction struck.

At that time, massive glaciations locked up huge amounts of water in an ice cap that covered parts of a large south polar landmass. The icy onslaught may have been triggered by the rise of North America's **Appalachian Mountains**. The large-scale weathering of these freshly uplifted rocks sucked carbon dioxide out of the atmosphere and drastically cooled the planet.

As a result, sea levels plummeted by hundreds of feet. Creatures living in shallow waters would have seen their habitats cool and shrink dramatically, dealing a major blow.

Whatever life remained recovered haltingly in chemically hostile waters. Once sea levels started to rise again, marine oxygen levels fell, which in turn caused ocean waters to more readily hold onto dissolved toxic metals.

Appalachian Mountains, USA

Devonian extinction
(375 Mya)

This extinction event eliminated about 80% of all species on Earth over a span of roughly 20 million years.

In several pulses across the Devonian, ocean levels dropped precipitously, which dealt serious blows to *conodonts* and ancient shelled relatives of squid and octopuses called *goniatites*. The worst of these pulses, called the **Kellwasser Event**, came around 372 million years ago. Rocks from the period in what is now Germany show that as oxygen levels plummeted, many reef-building creatures died out, including a major group of sea sponges called the *stromatoporoids*.

It is been hard to establish emphatically the cause for the late Devonian extinction pulses, but volcanism was a possible trigger. Within a couple million years of the **Kellwasser Event**, a large igneous province called the **Viluy Traps** ejected 240,000 cubic miles of lava over what is now Siberia. The eruption would have spewed greenhouse gases and sulphur dioxide, which can cause acid rain. Asteroids may also have contributed. Sweden's 32-mile-wide **Siljan crater**, one of Earth's biggest surviving impact craters, formed about 377 million years ago.

During the Devonian, plants underwent several important adaptations, including the stem-strengthening compound *lignin* and a full-fledged *vascular structure*. These traits allowed plants to get bigger - and for their roots to get deeper - than ever before. This would have had a significant effect on the increased rate of rock weathering.

The faster rocks weathered, the more excess nutrients flowed from land into the oceans. The influx would have triggered algae growth, and when these algae died, their decay removed oxygen from the oceans to form what are known as **anoxic dead zones**.

In addition, the spread of trees would have sucked CO_2 out of the atmosphere, potentially ushering in global cooling.

Not only did some creatures go extinct during the late Devonian, but species diversification slowed down during this time. The slowdown may have been caused by the global spread of invasive species.

As high sea levels led creatures from previously isolated marine habitats to mix, this led ecosystems around the world to somewhat normalize.

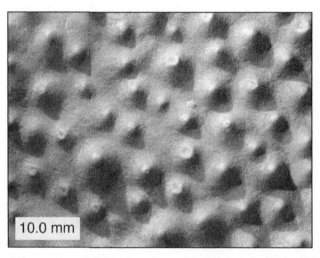

Stromatoporoid top view showing mamelons. Columbus Limestone (Devonian) of Kelleys Island, Ohio   PD

Conodont

Goniatite

Permian-Triassic extinction
252 - 251 Mya

Life on Earth faced the **'Great Dying'** at the time of the Permian-Triassic extinction. The cataclysm was the single worst event life on Earth has ever experienced. Over about 60,000 years, 96% of all marine species and about three of every four species on land died out. The world's forests were destroyed and did not come back in force until about 10 million years later. Of the five mass extinctions, the Permian-Triassic is the only one that annihilated large numbers of insect species. Marine ecosystems took four to eight million years to recover.

The extinction's single biggest cause is the **Siberian Traps**, an immense volcanic complex which again erupted, this time spreading more than 720,000 cubic miles of lava across what is now Siberia (*See Viluy Traps in Devonian extinction*). The eruption triggered the release of at least 14.5 trillion tons of carbon, more than 2.5 times what would be unleashed if every last ounce of fossil fuel on Earth were dug up and burned. What is more, magma from the Siberian Traps infiltrated coal basins on its way toward the surface, probably releasing even more greenhouse gases, notably methane.

In the immediate million years after the event, seawater and soil temperatures rose considerably. By 250.5 million years ago, sea surface temperatures at the Equator got as high as 40^0C.

As temperatures rose, rocks on land weathered more rapidly, hastened by **sulphuric acid rain** that formed from volcanic sulphur and rotting plants. Just as in the late Devonian, increased weathering would have brought on anoxia that suffocated the oceans. Climate models suggest that, at the time, the oceans lost an estimated 76% of their oxygen inventory. These models also suggest that the warming and oxygen loss account for most of the extinction's species losses.

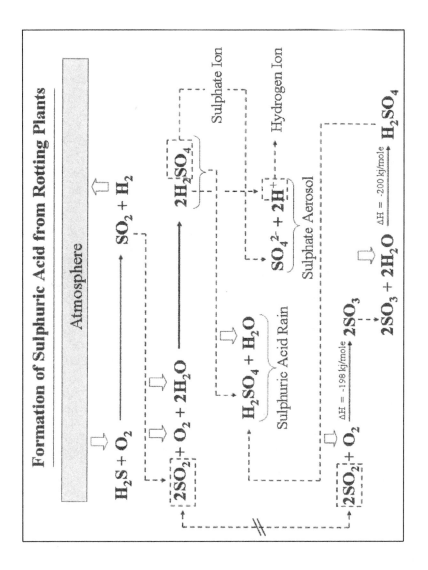

Formation of Sulphuric Acid from Rotting Plants

Methanosarcina

Methanosarcina is a genus of *euryarchaeote archaea* that
produces methane. These single-celled organisms are known
as anaerobic methanogens that produce methane using all three metabolic
pathways for methanogenesis. They live in diverse environments where
they can remain safe from the effects of oxygen, whether on the earth's
surface, in groundwater, in deep sea vents, and in animal digestive
tracts. *Methanosarcina* grow in colonies.

The amino acid *pyrrolysine* was first discovered in
a *Methanosarcina* species, *M. barkeri*. Primitive versions
of *hemoglobin* have been found in *M. acetivorans*, suggesting the microbe
or an ancestor of it may have played a crucial role in the evolution of life
on Earth. Species of *Methanosarcina* are also noted for unusually large
genomes. *M. acetivorans* has the largest known genome of any archaeon.

According to a theory published in 2014, *Methanosarcina* may have been
largely responsible for the largest extinction event in the Earth's history,
the **Permian–Triassic extinction event**. The theory suggests that
acquisition of a new metabolic pathway via gene transfer followed
by *exponential reproduction* allowed the microbe to rapidly consume vast
deposits of organic carbon in marine sediments, leading to a sharp buildup
of methane and carbon dioxide in the Earth's oceans and atmosphere that
killed around 90% of the world's species. This theory could better explain
the observed carbon isotope level in period deposits than other theories
such as volcanic activity.

Methanosarcina may be the only known *anaerobic methanogen* that
produces methane using all three known metabolic pathways
for **methanogenesis** and are capable of utilizing no less than nine
methanogenic substrates, including acetate.

Both *M. acetivorans* and *M. mazei* have exceptionally large genomes. As of August 2008, *M. acetivorans* possessed the largest sequenced archaeal genome with 5,751,492 base pairs. The genome of *M. mazei* has 4,096,345 base pairs.

In 2004, two primitive versions of hemoglobin were discovered in *M. acetivorans*. Known as *protoglobins*, these globins bind with oxygen much as hemoglobin does. In *M. acetivorans*, this allows for the removal of unwanted oxygen which would otherwise be toxic to this anaerobic organism. Protoglobins thus may have created a path for the evolution of later life-forms which are dependent on oxygen.

Following the **Great Oxygenation Event**, once there was free oxygen in Earth's atmosphere, the ability to process oxygen led to widespread radiation of life, and is one of the most fundamental stages in the evolution of Earth's lifeforms.

It was hypothesized that *Methanosarcina's* methane production may have been one of the causes of the **Permian–Triassic extinction event**. It is estimated that 70% of shell creatures died from ocean acidification, due to over-populated *Methanosarcina*. A study conducted by Chinese and American researchers supported that hypothesis. Using genetic analysis of about 50 *Methanosarcina* genomes, the team concluded that the microbe likely acquired the ability to efficiently consume acetate using acetat kinase and *phosphoacetyl transferase* roughly 240 ± 41 million years ago, about the time of the extinction event.

The scientists concluded that these new genes, combined with widely available organic carbon deposits in the ocean and a plentiful supply of nickel, allowed *Methanosarcina* populations to increase dramatically.

The scientists concluded that these new genes, combined with widely available organic carbon deposits in the ocean and a plentiful supply of nickel, allowed *Methanosarcina* populations to increase dramatically.

Under their theory, this led to the release of abundant methane as waste. Then, some of the methane would have been broken down into carbon dioxide by other organisms. The buildup of these two gases would have caused oxygen levels in the ocean to decrease dramatically, while also increasing acidity. Terrestrial climates would simultaneously have experienced rising temperatures and significant climate change from the release of these greenhouse gases into the atmosphere. It is possible the buildup of carbon dioxide and methane in the atmosphere eventually caused the release of hydrogen sulfide gas, further stressing terrestrial life.

Proceedings of the National Academy of Sciences in March 2014.

The microbe theory's proponents argue that it would better explain the rapid, but continual, rise of carbon isotope level in period sediment deposits than volcanic eruption, which causes a spike in carbon levels followed by a slow decline.

The microbe theory suggests that volcanic activity played a different role – supplying the nickel which *Methanosarcina* required as a cofactor. Thus, the microbe theory holds that Siberian volcanic activity was a catalyst for, but not the primary cause of the mass extinction.

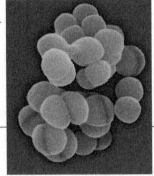

End Triassic extinction (200 Mya)

Life took a long time to recover from the **'Great Dying'**, but once it did, it diversified rapidly. Different reef-building creatures began to take hold, and lush vegetation covered the land, setting the stage for a group of reptiles called the *archosaurs*: the forerunners of birds, *crocodilians, pterosaurs,* and the non-avian dinosaurs. But about 200 million years ago, life endured another major blow and the sudden loss of up to 80% of species eliminated.

At the end of the Triassic, Earth warmed an average of between 12^0C and 15^0C, driven by a quadrupling of atmospheric CO_2 levels. This was probably triggered by huge amounts of greenhouse gases from the Central Atlantic Magmatic province, a large igneous province in central Pangaea, the supercontinent at the time. Remnants of those ancient lava flows are now split across eastern South America, eastern North America, and West Africa. The Central Atlantic Magmatic province was enormous. Its lava volume could cover the continental USA in a quarter-mile of rock.

The increase in CO_2 acidified the Triassic oceans, making it more difficult for marine creatures to build their shells from calcium carbonate. On land, the dominant vertebrates had been the *crocodilians*, which were bigger and far more diverse than they are today. Many of them died out. In their wake, the earliest dinosaurs, small, nimble creatures on the ecological periphery, rapidly diversified.

Cretaceous-Paleogene extinction (66 Mya)

The **Cretaceous-Paleogene (K-Pg)** extinction event is the most recent mass extinction and the only one definitively connected to a major asteroid impact. Some 75% of all species on the planet, including all non-avian dinosaurs, went extinct.

One day about 66 million years ago, an asteroid roughly 12 km across slammed into the waters off of what is now Mexico's **Yucatan Peninsula** at 72,000 kilometres an hour. The massive impact, which left a crater more than 193 miles wide, flung huge volumes of dust, debris, and sulphur into the atmosphere that brought on severe global cooling. Wildfires ignited any land within 1,450 km of the impact, and a huge tsunami rippled outward from the impact. Overnight, the ecosystems that supported non-avian dinosaurs began to collapse.

Global warming fuelled by volcanic eruptions at the **Deccan Traps** in India may have aggravated the event. Some scientists even argue that some of the **Deccan Traps** eruptions could have been triggered by the impact.

Deccan Traps, India

List of Mass Extinction Events

Period	Extinction	Date	Probable Cause
Quaternary	Holocene extinction	c. 10,000 BCE - Ongoing	Humans. Human induced catastrophes
Cretaceous	Cretaceous-Paleogene extinction event	66 Mya	Chicxulub impactor. The volcanism which resulted in the formation of the Deccan Traps may have contributed
Triassic	Triassic-Jurassic extinction event	201 Mya	Central Atlantic magmatic province. Impactor?
Permian	Permian-Triassic extinction event	252 Mya	Siberian Traps. Anoxic event. Ice Age
Permian	End-Capitanian extinction event*	260 Mya	Emeishan Traps
Devonian	Late Devonian extinction	375-360 Mya	Viluy Traps. Woodleigh impactor?
Ordovician	Ordovician-Silurian extinction events	450-440 Mya	Global cooling and sea level drop, possibly caused by a Gamma-ray burst or global warming related to volcanism and anoxia

*The End-Capitanian extinction event was an extinction event that occurred around 260 million years ago during a period of decreased species richness and increased extinction rates in the late Middle Permian during the Guadalupian epoch. It is also known as the end-Guadalupian extinction event because of its initial recognition between the Guadalupian and Lopingian series.

(All dates rounded

Extinction Intensity

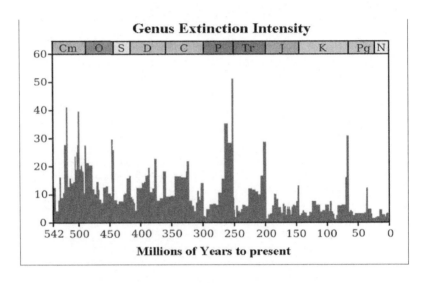

Genus Extinction Intensity

The above figure shows the genus extinction intensity, that is the fraction of genera that are present in each interval of time, but do not exist in the following interval. The data itself is taken from Rohde & Muller (2005, Supplementary Material), and are based on the Sepkoski's *Compendium of Marine Fossil Animal Genera* (2002). Note that these data do not represent all genera that have ever lived, but rather only a selection of marine genera whose qualities are such that they are easily preserved as fossils.

The two extinction events occurring in the Cambrian (Dresbachian and Botomian) are very large in percentage magnitude, but are not well known because of the relative scarcity of fossil producing life at that time.

The Middle Permian extinction is now argued by many to constitute a distinct extinction horizon, though the actual extinction amounts are sometimes lumped together with the End Permian extinctions.

As indicated, the Late Devonian extinction is actually resolvable into at least three distinct events spread over a period of ~40 million years. As these data are derived at the genus level, one can anticipate that the number of species extinctions is a higher percentage than shown.

Many of the extinction events appear to be somewhat extended in time. In at least some cases this is the result of a paleontological artefact known as the **Signor-Lipps effect** (Signor & Lipps 1982).

Briefly, this is the observation that inadequate sampling can cause a taxon to seem to disappear before its actual time of extinction. This has the effect of making an extinction event appear extended even if it occurred quite rapidly. Hence, when estimating the true magnitude of an extinction event it would be common to combine together the events occurring over several preceding bins as long as they also show excess extinctions.

This explains why many estimates of the magnitude of an extinction event may be larger than the 20-30% shown as the largest single bin for most of the extinctions.

Extinction today

Earth is currently experiencing a biodiversity crisis. Recent estimates suggest that extinction threatens up to a million species of plants and animals, in large part because of human activities such as deforestation, hunting, and over-fishing. Other serious threats include the spread of invasive species and diseases from human trade, as well as pollution and human-caused climate change.

Today, extinctions are occurring hundreds of times faster than they would naturally. If all species currently designated as critically endangered, endangered, or vulnerable go extinct in the next century, and if that rate of extinction continues without slowing down, we could approach the level of a mass extinction in as soon as 240 to 540 years.

Climate change presents a long-term threat. Humans' burning of fossil fuels has let us to chemically imitate large igneous provinces, through the injection of billions of tons of carbon dioxide and other gases into Earth's atmosphere each year. By total volume, past volcanoes emitted far more than humans do today. The **Siberian Traps** released more than 1,400 times the CO_2 than humans did in 2018 from burning fossil fuels for energy. However, humans are emitting greenhouse gases as fast as, or even faster than, the **Siberian Traps**, and Earth's climate is rapidly changing as a result.

As mass extinctions show us, sudden climate change can be profoundly disruptive. And while we have not yet crossed the 75% threshold of a mass extinction, that does not mean things are fine.

Well before hitting that grim marker, the damage would throw the ecosystems we call home into chaos, jeopardizing species around the world - **including us**!

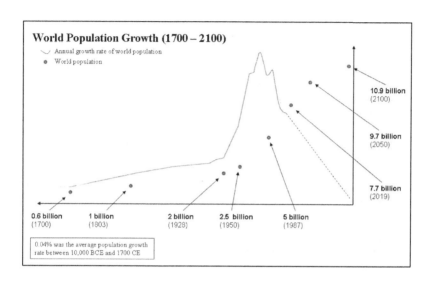

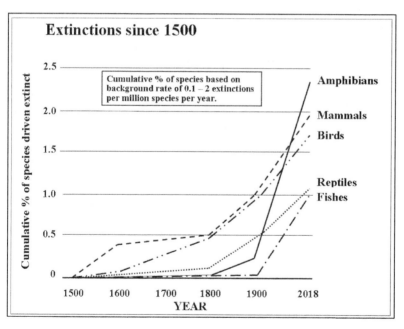

233

Malthusian Theory of Population

Thomas Robert Malthus (1766 –1834) believed that through preventative checks and positive checks, the population would be controlled to balance the food supply with the population level.

The **Malthusian Theory of Population** is the theory of exponential population and arithmetic food supply growth. The theory was proposed by Malthus. who believed that a balance between population growth and food supply can be established through preventive and positive checks.

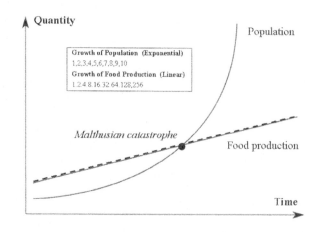

234

Through various improvements and economies made in living conditions and food production, the point at which is inferred to as the 'Malthusian Catastrophe' was not reached - that is until the late 1980s.

The graph below reflects the fact that from around this time there has been a general increasing shortage of food against an ever rising growth in population.

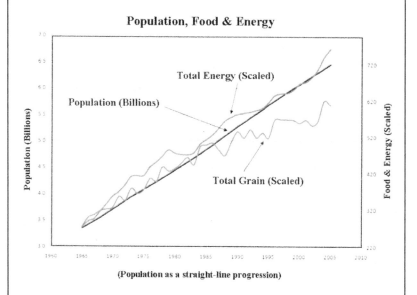

(Population as a straight-line progression)

Malthus was somewhat prophetic in stating that, unless preventative and positive checks were instigated, then this would result in famine, pestilence and war.

Evolution and Global Warming

One of the key mechanisms of evolution, **natural selection**, causes organisms to evolve in response to a changing environment. Imagine a population with several different variants in it: some individuals happen to be better able to survive and reproduce at higher temperatures than other individuals. Clearly, if the temperature increases, those heat tolerant individuals will have an advantage and will leave more offspring, and those offspring will also carry the genes for heat tolerance. Over many generations, this process produces a population with adaptations well-suited for the hotter environment. So long as the population has different genetic variants in it, some better able to survive and reproduce in particular situations than others, the population has the capacity to evolve when faced with a changing environment.

According to the 2020 Annual Climate Report of the **National Oceanic and Atmospheric Administration (NOAA)** in the USA, the combined land and ocean temperature has increased at an average rate of $0.08°C$ per decade since 1880. However, the average rate of increase since 1981 of $0.18°C$ has been more than twice that rate.

As insignificant as this change may appear, this is more than enough to change the ecology and evolution of life on Earth. In many cases, these changes are simply non-evolutionary but there have been cases where it has been established beyond doubt that species have actually evolved in response to global warming. These include Coral, Canadian squirrels, European great tits and blackcaps, and North American mosquitoes.

Whereas small animals like these have the ability to evolve along with the changing environment, larger species often have far longer generation times and smaller population sizes.

Consequently, genetic changes would not allow for the adaptations to keep up with environmental changes and be faced with inevitable extinction.

Greenhouse Effect

While other planets in the Solar System are either extremely hot or bitterly cold, Earth's surface has relatively mild, stable temperatures. Earth enjoys these temperatures because of its atmosphere, which is the thin layer of gases that cloak and protect the planet. In fact, if there was no water vapour, the average temperature of Earth would be about 19°C cooler overall.

It is generally agreed now that humans have changed Earth's atmosphere in dramatic ways over the past two centuries, resulting in global warming. To understand global warming though, it is first necessary to become familiar with the **greenhouse effect**.

There is a delicate balancing act occurring every day all across the Earth, involving the radiation the planet receives from space and the radiation that is reflected back out to space. Earth is constantly bombarded with enormous amounts of radiation, primarily from the Sun. This solar radiation strikes the Earth's atmosphere in the form of visible light, plus ultraviolet (UV), infrared (IR) and other types of radiation that are invisible to the human eye. UV radiation has a shorter wavelength and a higher energy level than visible light, while IR radiation has a longer wavelength and a weaker energy level. It is estimated that about 30% of the radiation striking Earth's atmosphere is immediately reflected back out to space by clouds, ice, snow, sand and other reflective surfaces.
This is referred to as the **'albedo effect'**. The remaining 70% of incoming solar radiation is absorbed by the oceans, the land and the atmosphere. As they heat up, the oceans, land and

atmosphere release heat in the form of IR thermal radiation, which passes out of the atmosphere and into space. It is this equilibrium of incoming and outgoing radiation that makes the Earth habitable, with an average temperature of about 15^0C.

Without this atmospheric equilibrium, Earth would be as cold and lifeless as its moon, or as blazing hot as Venus. The moon, which has almost no atmosphere, is about minus 153^0C on its dark side. Venus, on the other hand, has a very dense atmosphere that traps solar radiation; the average temperature on Venus is about 462^0C.

The exchange of incoming and outgoing radiation that warms the Earth is often referred to as the **greenhouse effect** because a greenhouse works in much the same way.

Carbon dioxide (CO_2) and other greenhouse gases act like a blanket, absorbing IR radiation and preventing it from escaping into outer space. The net effect is the gradual heating of Earth's atmosphere and surface, a process known as **global warming**.

These greenhouse gases include:

- Water vapour   (H_2O)
- Carbon dioxide   (CO_2)
- Methane   (CH_4)
- Nitrous oxide   (N_2O)
- Carbon monoxide   (CO)
- and other gases.

Since the dawn of the **Industrial Revolution** in the 1750's, the burning of fossil fuels like coal, oil and gasoline have greatly increased the concentration of greenhouse gases in the atmosphere, especially CO_2.
Deforestation is arguably the second largest anthropogenic source of carbon dioxide to the atmosphere ranging between 6% and 17 %.

Atmospheric CO_2 levels have increased by more than 40% since the beginning of the Industrial Revolution, from about 280 parts per million (ppm) in the 1800s to 400 ppm today. The last time Earth's atmospheric levels of CO_2 reached 400 ppm was during the Pliocene, between 5 million and 3 million years ago.

The **greenhouse effect**, combined with increasing levels of greenhouse gases and the resulting global warming, is expected to have profound implications. If global warming continues unchecked, it will cause significant climate change, a rise in sea levels, increasing ocean acidification, extreme weather events and other severe natural and societal impacts. And have a devastating effect on Earth's future evolution. Yet CO_2 gas is **not** the only greenhouse gas.

As already stated, water vapour is considered a **necessary** greenhouse gas; without it, life on Earth would be very different. For this reason, it is not usually considered when looking at the effects of global warming. Earth therefore has a natural greenhouse effect, but this is being put out of balance by the various anthropomorphic effects, notably from those gases mentioned above.

Atmospheric lifetime and GWP relative to CO_2 at different time horizons for various greenhouse gases

Gas name	Chemical formula	Lifetime (years)	Global warming potential (GWP) for given time horizon		
			20-yr	100-yr	500-yr
Carbon dioxide	CO_2	Variable	1	1	1
Methane	CH_4	12	72	25	7.6
Nitrous oxide	N_2O	114	289	298	153
CFC-12	CCl_2F_2	100	11 000	10 900	5 200
HCFC-22	$CHClF_2$	12	5 160	1 810	549
Tetrafluoromethane	CF_4	50 000	5 210	7 390	11 200
Hexafluoroethane	C_2F_6	10 000	8 630	12 200	18 200
Sulphur hexafluoride	SF_6	3 200	16 300	22 800	32 600
Nitrogen trifluoride	NF_3	740	12 300	17 200	20 700

It is not strictly true that the 16% of the oxygen being produced on LAND today is from photosynthesis in the Amazon forest, as has been stated.

The Amazon forest, just like any other ecosystem, ends up consuming nearly all of the oxygen it makes.

Plants use about **half or more** of the oxygen they produce as they, like other cellular organisms, respire using the oxygen to break down carbohydrates to grow and survive in the inverse reaction to photosynthesis.

People associate respiration with animals, but plants do it too. It's just not usually detectable until night-time, when plants have stopped releasing oxygen.

Origin of Water on Earth

The **origin of water on Earth** is the subject of a body of research in the fields of planetary science, astronomy, and astrobiology. Earth is unique among the rocky planets in the Solar System in that it is the only planet known to have oceans of liquid water on its surface. Liquid water, which is necessary for life as we know it, continues to exist on the surface of Earth because the planet is at a distance, known as the **habitable (or Goldilocks) zone**, far enough from the Sun that it does not lose its water to the runaway **Greenhouse Effect**, but not so far that low temperatures cause all water on the planet to freeze.

It was long thought that Earth's water did not originate from the planet's region of the protoplanetary disk. Instead, it was hypothesized water and other volatiles must have been delivered to Earth from the outer Solar System later in its history. Recent research, however, indicates that hydrogen inside the Earth played a role in the formation of the ocean. The two ideas are not mutually exclusive, as there is also evidence that water was delivered to Earth by impacts from icy planetesimals similar in composition to asteroids in the outer edges of the asteroid belt.

One factor in estimating when water appeared on Earth is that water is continually being lost to space. Water molecules in the atmosphere are broken up by photolysis, and the resulting free hydrogen atoms can sometimes escape Earth's gravitational pull. When the Earth was younger and less massive, water would have been lost to space more easily. Lighter elements like hydrogen and helium are expected to leak from the atmosphere continually, but isotopic ratios of heavier noble gases in the modern atmosphere suggest that even the heavier elements in the early atmosphere were subject to significant losses. In particular, xenon is useful for calculations of water loss over time. Not only is it a noble gas (and therefore is not removed from the atmosphere through chemical reactions with other elements), but comparisons between abundances of its nine stable isotopes in the modern atmosphere reveal that the Earth lost at least one ocean of water early in its history, between the Hadean and Archean.

Any water on Earth during the later part of its accretion would have been disrupted by the Moon-forming impact (~4.5 billion years ago), which likely vaporized much of Earth's crust and upper mantle and created a rock-vapour atmosphere around the young planet. The rock vapour would have condensed within two thousand years, leaving behind hot volatiles which probably resulted in a majority carbon dioxide atmosphere with hydrogen and water vapour. Afterwards, liquid water oceans may have existed despite the surface temperature of 230°C due to the increased atmospheric pressure of the CO_2 rich atmosphere. As cooling continued, most CO_2 was removed from the atmosphere by *subduction* and *dissolution* in ocean water.

There is also geological evidence that helps constrain the time frame for liquid water existing on Earth. A sample of pillow basalt (a type of rock formed during an underwater eruption) was recovered from the **Isua Greenstone Belt**, south western Greenland and provides evidence that water existed on Earth 3.7 -3.8 billion years ago.

In the **Nuvvuagittuq Greenstone Belt**, Quebec, Canada, rocks dated at 3.750 billion years old by one study and 4.288 billion years old by another show evidence of the presence of water at these ages. If oceans existed earlier than this, any geological evidence either has yet to be discovered or has since been destroyed by geological processes like *crustal recycling*. More recently, in August 2020, researchers reported that sufficient water to fill the oceans may have always been on the Earth since the beginning of the planet's formation.

Unlike rocks, minerals called *zircons* are highly resistant to weathering and geological processes and so are used to understand conditions on the very early Earth.

Mineralogical evidence from *zircons* has shown that liquid water and an atmosphere must have existed 4.404 ± 0.008 billion years ago, very soon after the formation of Earth.

This presents somewhat of a paradox, as the cool early Earth hypothesis suggests temperatures were cold enough to freeze water between about 4.4 billion and 4.0 billion years ago. Other studies of zircons found in Australian Hadean rock point to the existence of **plate tectonics** as early as 4 billion years ago. If true, that implies that rather than a hot, molten surface and an atmosphere full of CO_2, early Earth's surface was much as it is today. The action of **plate tectonics** traps vast amounts of CO_2, thereby reducing greenhouse effects, and leading to a much cooler surface temperature, and the formation of solid rock and liquid water.

Earth's Water Inventory

While the majority of Earth's surface is covered by oceans, those oceans make up just a small fraction of the mass of the planet, which is 0.023% of the total mass of Earth, 6.0×10^{24} kg. An additional 5.0×10^{20} kg of water is estimated to exist in ice, lakes, rivers, groundwater, and atmospheric water vapour. A significant amount of water is also stored in Earth's crust, mantle, and core. Unlike molecular H_2O that is found on the surface, water in the interior exists primarily in hydrated mineral or as trace amounts of hydrogen bonded to oxygen atoms in **anhydrous minerals**. Hydrated silicates on the surface transport water into the mantle at **convergent plate boundaries**, where oceanic crust is subducted underneath **continental crust**. While it is difficult to estimate the total water content of the mantle due to limited samples, approximately three times the mass of the Earth's oceans could be stored there.

How did Water get on Earth?

About 70% of the surface of our planet Earth is covered in water. We are nestled in our solar system at just the right distance from the Sun for this liquid water to exist, any farther and that water would be frozen in ice. Any closer and temperatures would be too hot and we would be at risk for a runaway greenhouse effect similar to what's happening on the scorching surface of Venus. Our not-too-cold, not-too-hot position in the so-called '**Goldilocks Zone**' is a pretty good thing because, of course, water is necessary for life.

But how did that water get here? Water is a defining characteristic of our planet and it plays such an important part of our daily lives. Understanding how water arrived on Earth is a key part of understanding how and when life evolved here as well. But we do not even know how it where it came from. Scientists are still actively researching how our planet got to be so wet in the first place.

Our current picture of planet formation starts with a protoplanetary disk. That is a large disk of gas and dust swirling around our newly-formed Sun. As the grains of dust and ice in the disk interact with themselves, those grains begin to form bigger and bigger clumps. Eventually those clumps form what we call planetesimals, the building blocks of rocky and giant planets.

But in the early period of our solar system's formation, that disk was much hotter at the position where our Earth sits now. So even though there was most likely water molecules present in the mess of debris that made up the disk, it was too hot for water to condense into a liquid, causing it to evaporate instead.

What is more, the early Earth did not then have an atmosphere making it easier for any liquid water droplets to be blown off into space.

This leaves us with a bit of a puzzle. If the Earth could not have formed from the disk with its oceans already intact, how did they get here?

If Earth's water wasn't formed along with the Earth, then, planetary scientists suspect, it must have been delivered later via extraterrestrial messenger. Both asteroids and comets visit the Earth *and* are known to harbour ice. In fact, models of the compositions of asteroids and comets suggest that they even harbour enough ice to have delivered an amount of water equal to Earth's oceans.

So, problem solved? Not quite. Was it a comet or an asteroid that brought Earth's water? Was it a single event, or many? And how long ago did this happen?

One way to determine whether an asteroid or a comet brought us our oceans is to look at the chemical make-up of these cosmic objects and compare that make-up to the Earth to see which are more alike.

For example, a water molecule always has 10 protons (8 from its oxygen molecule and one each from its hydrogen molecules) and usually has 8 neutrons (from the oxygen molecule only). But different isotopes of water may have extra neutrons. Heavy water, for example, is what we call water made from oxygen and deuterium, which is an isotope of hydrogen, or just hydrogen with an added neutron.

One study published in the journal *Science* in 2014 looked at the relative amounts of different isotopes of water - water molecules with varying numbers of neutrons - on meteorites believed to have fallen to Earth from the ancient asteroid **Vesta**. This asteroid is the second largest object in the Asteroid Belt and has a heavily cratered surface suggesting a violent past full of collisions.

The **Vesta** rock samples had the *same* distribution of isotopes seen on Earth. Now, that does not mean that **Vesta** was necessarily the source of our water but that an object or objects similar to Vesta in age and in composition could be responsible.

But the dispute is still far from settled. For a while, studies of comets seemed to back up the idea that Earth's water came from asteroids. The recent **Rosetta** spacecraft was the first to orbit a comet and then also the first to send a lander (called **Philae**) to the comet's surface. Thanks to **Rosetta** and **Philae**, scientists discovered that the ratio of heavy water (water made from deuterium) to 'regular' water (made from regular old hydrogen) on comets was different from that on Earth, suggesting that, at most, 10% of Earth's water could have originated on a comet.

However, in 2018, a close passage of the comet **46P/Wirtanen** allowed planetary scientists a more detailed look at its isotopic make-up using **SOFIA**, a jumbo jet with a telescope on board. They found the comet had similar ratios of deuterium and hydrogen as those found on Earth.

What made this comet different from the one studied by **Rosetta** and **Philae** was that comet **46P/Wirtanen** comes from a class of what are known as '*hyperactive*' comets, meaning they release more water as they draw closer to the Sun than a regular comet does.

As a standard comet nears the heat of the Sun, the ice particles from its nucleus sublimate or go directly from solid ice to a gas, which can then condense later into liquid water if it were, say, to arrive on a planet's surface. But a *hyperactive* comet loses not only the ice from its nucleus but also ice-rich particles in its atmosphere that were previously heated and released from the nucleus but still hang around. Those icy particles may be what make *hyperactive* comets have isotope ratios more similar to those on Earth.

Approximate number of water molecules in all oceans of the world	
The approximate total volume of all seas and oceans on Earth:	$1.37 \times 10^9 /km^3$
The average density of seawater:	$1023.6 \ kg/m^3$
This means that the total mass of water in all oceans:	$1.40 \times 10^{21} \ kg.$
The number of moles is then:	$7.8 \times 10^{22} \ mol.$
1 mol contains 6.02×10^{23} molecules (Avogadro's constant)	
This means that the number of molecules in all oceans equals:	$6.02 \times 10^{23} * 7.8 \times 10^{22} = \underline{\mathbf{4.7 \times 10^{46}}}$
(give or take several orders of magnitude)	

(4,700,000,000,000,000,000,000,000,000,000,000,000,000,000,000 molecules)

Main Properties of Water

But what makes water so special and such an essential component together with those that are seen to be vital in supporting life as we know it on Earth?

Essentially, the following properties are those that make water a singularly special compound:

Attraction to Other Polar Molecules:

Cohesion

Water's polarity lends it to be attracted to other water molecules. The hydrogen bonds in water hold other water molecules together.

Due to water's cohesiveness:

- Liquid water has surface tension. This allows for insects, such as Water Striders, to walk on water.

- Water is a liquid at moderate temperatures, and not a gas.

Adhesion

- Water's attraction between molecules of a different substance is called adhesion. Water is adhesive to any molecule it can form hydrogen bonds with.

- Capillary action occurs.

High-Specific Heat Capacity

Water can moderate temperature because of the two properties: high-specific heat and the high heat of vaporization.

High-specific heat is the amount of energy that is absorbed or lost by one gram of a substance to change the temperature by 1 degree Celsius. Water molecules form a lot of hydrogen bonds between one another. In turn, a lot of energy is needed to break down those bonds. Breaking the bonds allows individual water molecules to move freely about and have a higher temperature.

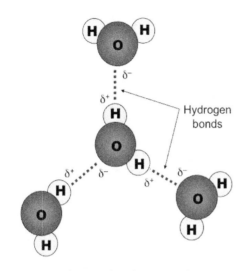

In other words: if there are a lot of individual water molecules moving about, they will create more friction and more heat, which means a higher temperature.

The hydrogen bonds between water molecules absorb the heat when they break and release heat when they form, which minimizes temperature changes.

Water helps maintain a moderate temperature of organisms and environments.

Water takes a long time to heat up, and holds its temperature longer when heat is not applied.

Enthalpy of Evaporation

Water's high enthalpy of evaporation is basically the amount of heat energy needed to change a gram of liquid into gas.

Water also needs a lot of energy in order to break down the hydrogen bonds.

The evaporation of water off a surface causes a cooling effect.

Lower Density of Ice

At cooler temperatures, the hydrogen bonds of water molecules form ice crystals. The hydrogen bonds are more stable and will maintain its crystal-like shape.

Ice, the solid form of water, is less dense than water because of the hydrogen bonds being spaced out and being relatively apart.

The low density is what allows icebergs to float and are the reason that only the top part of lakes is frozen.

High Polarity

Water is a polar molecule that has a high level of polarity and attraction to ions and other polar molecules.

Insofar as water can form hydrogen bonds, this makes it a powerful solvent. Water molecules are attracted to other molecules that contain a full charge, like an ion, a partial charge, or polar.

Salt (Na^+Cl^-) dissolves in water. Water molecules surround the salt molecules and separate the Na^+ from the Cl^- by forming hydration shells around those two individual ions.

NaCl crystal structure   NaCl in water

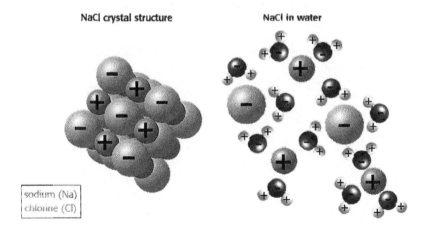

sodium (Na)
chlorine (Cl)

Carbon dioxide

Carbon dioxide (CO_2) is a colourless, odourless non-flammable gas and is the most prominent greenhouse gas in Earth's atmosphere. This gas stays in the atmosphere for up to 1,000 years.

It is recycled through the atmosphere by the natural process of **photosynthesis**, which makes human life possible. Carbon dioxide is emitted into the air as humans exhale, burns fossil fuels for energy, and deforests the planet.

Every year humans add **over 30 billion tons** of carbon dioxide into the atmosphere by these processes, and it has increased by 30% since 1750.

CO_2 Concentration in Parts per Million

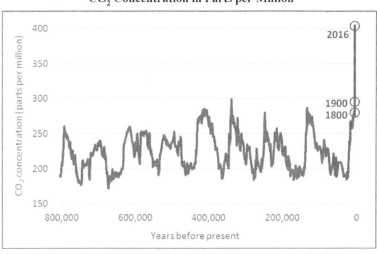

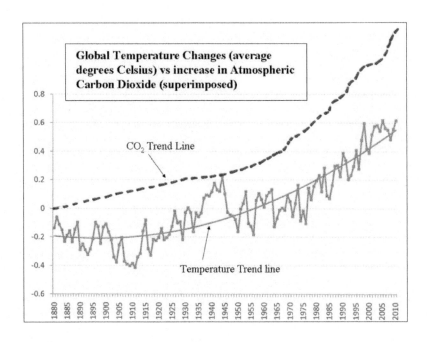

Global Temperature Changes (average degrees Celsius) vs increase in Atmospheric Carbon Dioxide (superimposed)

CO_2 Trend Line

Temperature Trend line

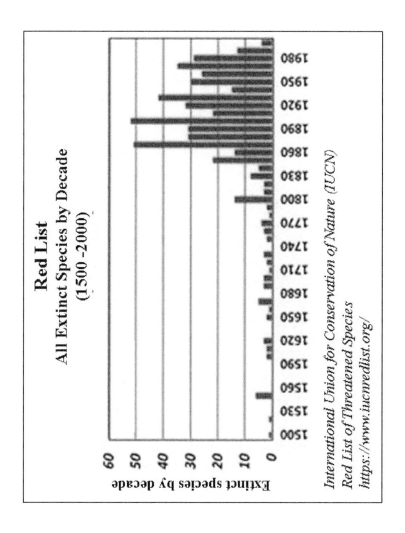

Red List
All Extinct Species by Decade
(1500 -2000)

Extinct species by decade

International Union for Conservation of Nature (IUCN)
Red List of Threatened Species
https://www.iucnredlist.org/

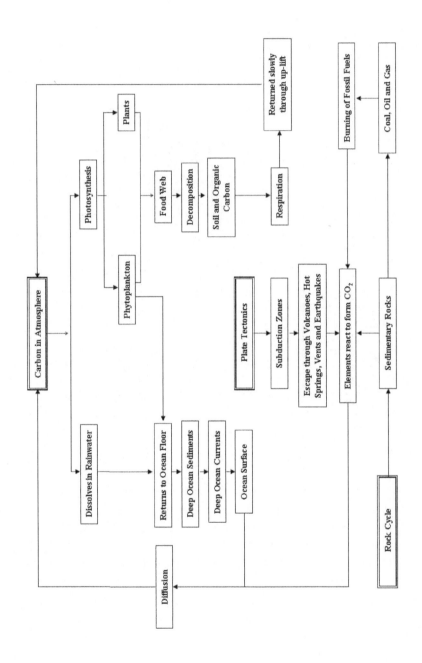

Methane

Methane is an important greenhouse gas with a **Global Warming Potential (GWP)** of 25 compared to CO_2 (potential of 1) over a 100-year period and 72 over a 20-year period.

In 2010, methane levels in the Arctic were measured at 1850 nmol/mol. This level is over twice as high as at any time in the last 400,000 years. The Earth's atmospheric methane concentration has increased by about 150% since 1750.

The **Intergovernmental Panel on Climate Change (IPCC)** has stated that *"Observed increases in well-mixed greenhouse gas concentrations since around 1750 are unequivocally caused by human activities"*. From 2015 to 2019 sharp rises in levels of atmospheric methane have continued to be recorded.

Climate change can increase atmospheric methane levels by increasing methane production in natural ecosystems, forming what is referred to as a **climate change feedback**.

The combustion of methane is a **multiple step reaction** which is summarized as follows:

$$CH_4 + 2O_2 \rightarrow CO_2 + 2H_2O$$
$$(\Delta H = -891 \text{ kJ/mol})$$

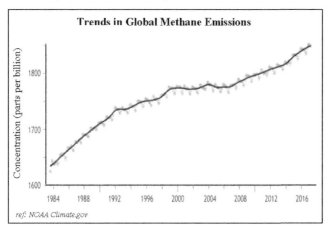

255

Methane is a *'naturally occurring organic compound'*, but human activity has increased the amount of this potent greenhouse gas that goes into the atmosphere. Most of the methane that humans emit comes from natural gas, landfills, coal mining and manure.

The amount of methane a dam could release varies depending on where and how the dam was built. It has been found that the mud behind one dam in Washington, USA released 36 times more methane than normal when water levels were low.

The gas is also escaping from underneath Arctic ice and permafrost due to global warming. Methane gas, which had been trapped under the ice, is now escaping into the atmosphere as the Arctic region heats up. This, in turn, could speed up further warming.

As much as 4 percent of the planet's methane comes from the ocean. According to scientists from the University of Illinois and Institute for Genomic Biology, the ocean-based microbe *Nitrosopumilus maritimus* produces methane through a complex biochemical process.

Rice may be one of the biggest food staples around the world, but its cultivation produced the third-highest levels of methane from all agricultural processes in 2010, according to an EPA report.

Rice is grown in flooded fields, a situation that depletes the soil of oxygen. Soils that are anoxic allow the bacteria that produce methane from decomposing organic matter to thrive. Some of this methane then bubbles to the surface, but most of it is diffused back into the atmosphere through the rice plants themselves.

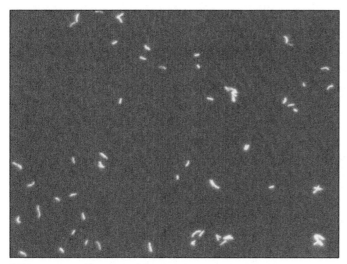

Nitrosopumilus maritimus

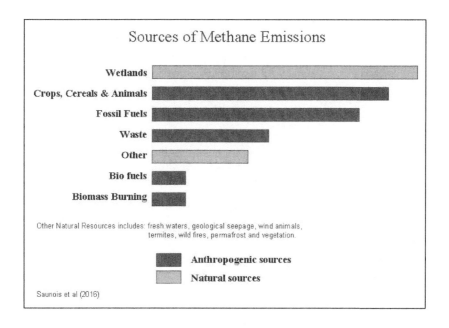

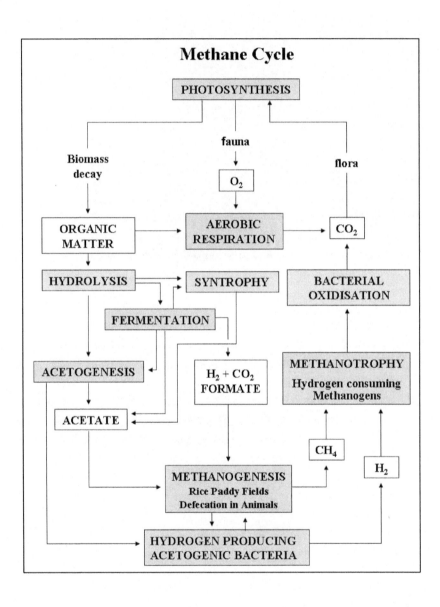

Methane Cycle

Nitrous oxide

Nitrous oxide's atmospheric concentration reached 333 parts per billion (ppb) in 2020, increasing at a rate of about 1 ppb annually. It is a major scavenger of stratospheric ozone, with an impact comparable to that of CFCs.

Global accounting of N_2O sources and sinks over the decade ending 2016 indicates that about 40% of the average 17 TgN/yr (teragrams of Nitrogen per year) of emissions originated from human activity, and shows that emissions growth chiefly came from expanding agriculture and industry sources within emerging economies.

Being the third most important long-lived greenhouse gas, nitrous oxide also substantially contributes to global warming.

Nitrous oxide is a minor component of Earth's atmosphere and is an active part of the planetary nitrogen cycle. Based on analysis of air samples gathered from sites around the world, its concentration surpassed 330 ppb in 2017. The growth rate of about 1 ppb per year has also accelerated during recent decades. Nitrous oxide's atmospheric abundance has grown more than 20% from a base level of about 270 ppb in year 1750.

Aquatint depiction of a laughing gas (Nitrous oxide) party in the nineteenth century, by Thomas Rowlandson

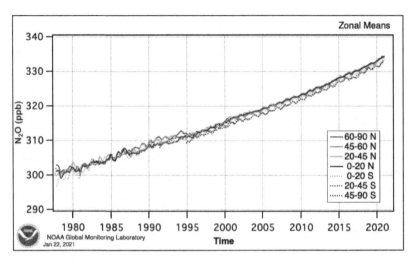

Nitrous oxide atmospheric concentration since 1978. PD

Carbon monoxide

Though **carbon monoxide** does not cause climate change directly, its presence affects the abundance of greenhouse gases such as methane and carbon dioxide. Carbon monoxide is short-lived in the atmosphere (with an average lifetime of about one to two months); Carbon monoxide is a colourless, odourless, tasteless gas. It is also flammable and is quite toxic to humans and other oxygen-breathing organisms.

Carbon monoxide (CO) is present in small amounts (about 100 ppb) in the Earth's atmosphere. Most of the rest comes from chemical reactions with organic compounds emitted by human activities and natural origins due to photochemical reactions in the troposphere that generate about 5×10^{12} kilograms per year. Other natural sources of CO include volcanoes, forest and bushfires fires, and miscellaneous other forms of combustion such as fossil fuels.

Small amounts are also emitted from the ocean and from geological activity because carbon monoxide occurs dissolved in molten volcanic rock at high pressures in the Earth's <u>mantle</u>. Because natural sources of carbon monoxide are so variable from year to year, it is difficult to accurately measure natural emissions of the gas.

Natural sources of carbon monoxide in Earth's atmosphere include volcanoes and bushfires. Volcanic gases contain between 0.01 and 2% carbon monoxide. Humans contribute vast quantities of CO to our atmosphere, mostly as a result of automobile emissions. Certain industrial processes, along with fossil fuel and biomass burning, are major human-produced sources of CO.

Carbon monoxide is a relatively unreactive compound, so it does not pose much threat to plants or exposed materials. However, the gas is quite poisonous to humans and other air-breathing creatures that need oxygen.

Carbon monoxide is often a product of incomplete combustion. If there is too little oxygen, or too much carbon, present when something burns, the burning produces carbon monoxide (CO) instead of (or as well as) carbon dioxide (CO_2).

Example – Burning of Methane (CH_4)

Complete Combustion:

$$CH_4 + 2O_2 \longrightarrow CO_2 + 2H_2O + energy$$

Incomplete Combustion:

$$4CH_4 + 7O_2 \longrightarrow 2CO + 2CO_2 + 8H_2O$$

Carbon monoxide indirectly contributes to the build-up of some greenhouse gases in the troposphere. It reacts with certain chemicals that would otherwise destroy methane and ozone, thus helping to elevate the concentrations of methane and ozone.

Carbon monoxide is found beyond Earth as well. It has been detected in gaseous nebulae, in the atmospheres of other planets, and in the ice of comets.

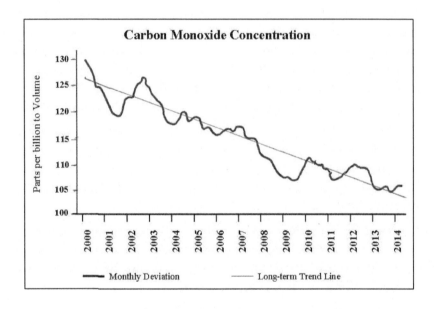

Ammonia

Ammonia is **not** a greenhouse gases, but they do negatively impacts on human and animal health while also damaging ecosystems. Ammonia is a gaseous form of nitrogen; the main ways in which it is lost in agriculture are the storage and application of organic manures, chemical fertiliser applications and grazing animals. **Ammonia** is a compound of nitrogen and hydrogen with the formula NH_3. A stable binary hydride, and the simplest nitrogen hydride, ammonia is a colourless gas with a distinct pungent smell. Biologically, it is a common nitrogenous waste, particularly among aquatic organisms, and it contributes significantly to the nutritional needs of terrestrial organisms by serving as a precursor to 45% of the world's food and fertilizers.

Ammonia, either directly or indirectly, is also a building block for the synthesis of many pharmaceutical products and is used in many commercial cleaning products. It is mainly collected by downward displacement of both air and water.

Although common in nature – both terrestrially and in the outer planets of the Solar System – and in wide use, ammonia is both caustic and hazardous in its concentrated form. In many countries it is classified as an extremely hazardous substance, and is subject to strict reporting requirements by facilities which produce, store, or use it in significant quantities.

The global industrial production of ammonia in 2018 was 175 million tonnes, with no significant change relative to the 2013 global industrial production of 175 million tonnes. Industrial ammonia is sold either as ammonia liquor (usually 28% ammonia in water) or as pressurized or refrigerated anhydrous liquid ammonia transported in tank cars or cylinders.

NH_3 boils at -33.34^0 C at a pressure of one atmosphere, so the liquid must be stored under pressure or at low temperature.

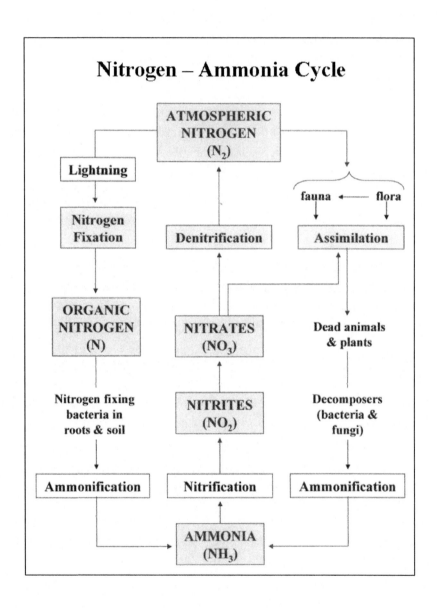

Nitrogen – Ammonia Cycle

ATMOSPHERIC NITROGEN (N_2)

Lightning

Nitrogen Fixation

Denitrification

Assimilation

fauna ← flora

ORGANIC NITROGEN (N)

NITRATES (NO_3)

Dead animals & plants

Nitrogen fixing bacteria in roots & soil

NITRITES (NO_2)

Decomposers (bacteria & fungi)

Ammonification

Nitrification

Ammonification

AMMONIA (NH_3)

Hydrogen sulphide

Hydrogen sulphide is not a Greenhouse gas, but is a colorless chalcogen-hydride gas which is toxic to humans and most other animals by inhibiting cellular respiration a manner similar to hydrogen cyanide. Despite this, the human body produces small amounts of this sulphide and its mineral salts.

Hydrogen sulphide is often produced from the microbial breakdown of organic matter in the absence of oxygen, such through anaerobic digestion, which is done by sulphate-reducing bacteria and other microorganisms. Significantly, it also occurs in volcanoes, natural gas deposits and hot springs where it probably arises via the hydrolysis of sulphide minerals:

$$MS + H_2O \rightarrow MO + H_2S.$$

Hydrogen sulphide can be present naturally in water, often as a result of the action of sulphate-reducing bacteria.

The Sulphur Cycle

Hydrogen sulphide is a central participant in the **Sulphur Cycle**. In the absence of oxygen, sulphur-reducing and sulphate-reducing bacteria derive energy from oxidizing hydrogen or organic molecules by reducing elemental sulphur or sulphate to hydrogen sulphide. Other bacteria liberate hydrogen sulphide from sulphur-containing amino acids.

Several groups of bacteria can use hydrogen sulphide as fuel, oxidizing it to elemental sulphur or to sulphate by using dissolved oxygen, metal oxides (e.g. iron oxyhydroxides and manganese oxides), or nitrate as electron acceptors.

The purple sulphur bacteria and the green sulphur bacteria use hydrogen sulphide as an electron donor in photosynthesis, thereby producing elemental sulphur.

This mode of photosynthesis is older than the mode of cyanobacteria, algae, and plants, which uses water as electron donor and liberates oxygen.

The biochemistry of hydrogen sulphide is a key part of the chemistry of the iron-sulphur world. In this model of the origin of life on Earth, geologically produced hydrogen sulphide is postulated as an electron donor driving the reduction of carbon dioxide.

Interstellar and Planetary Occurrence

Hydrogen sulphide has often been detected in the interstellar medium. It also occurs in the clouds of planets in our solar system.

Mass Extinctions

Hydrogen sulphide has been implicated in several mass extinctions that have occurred in the Earth's past. In particular, a buildup of hydrogen sulphide in the atmosphere may have caused, or at least contributed to, the Permian-Triassic extinction event 252 million years ago.

Organic residues from these extinction boundaries indicate that the oceans were anoxic and had species of shallow plankton that metabolized hydrogen sulphide. The formation of this gas may have been initiated by massive volcanic eruptions, which emitted carbon dioxide and methane into the atmosphere, which warmed the oceans, lowering their capacity to absorb oxygen that would otherwise oxidize hydrogen sulphide. The increased levels of hydrogen sulphide could have killed oxygen-generating plants as well as depleted the ozone layer, causing further stress.

Evidence in Modern Times

Small Hydrogen sulphide blooms have been detected in modern times in the Dead Sea and in the Atlantic Ocean off the coast of Namibia.

Hydrogen Sulphide Eruptions

"Ocean waters glowed peacock green off the northern Namibian coast in late November 2010. The Moderate Resolution Imaging Spectroradiometer (**MODIS**) on NASA's **Terra** satellite captured this natural-colour image on 21st November, 2010.

These bright swirls of green occur along a continental shelf bustling with biological activity. Phytoplankton blooms often occur along coastlines where nutrient-rich waters well up from ocean depths. The light colour of this ocean water suggests the calcite plating of *coccolithophores*.

Farther south along the coast of Namibia, hydrogen sulphide eruptions occur fairly frequently. According to a study published in 2009, ocean currents deliver **oxygen-poor water** from the north, while the bacteria that break down phytoplankton also consume oxygen, depleting the supply even more. In this oxygen-poor environment, anaerobic bacteria produce hydrogen sulphide gas. When the hydrogen sulphide finally reaches oxygen-rich surface waters, pure sulphur precipitates into the water. The sulphur's yellow mixes with the deep blue ocean to make bright green.

So this swirl of bright green could contain *phytoplankton*, sulphur, or a combination of the two".

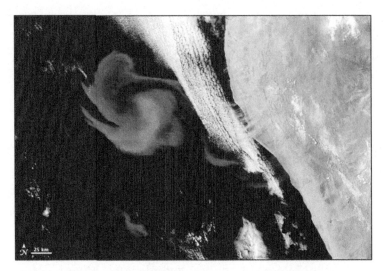

ref: MODIS Land Rapid Response Team at NASA GSFC. Caption by Michon Scott.

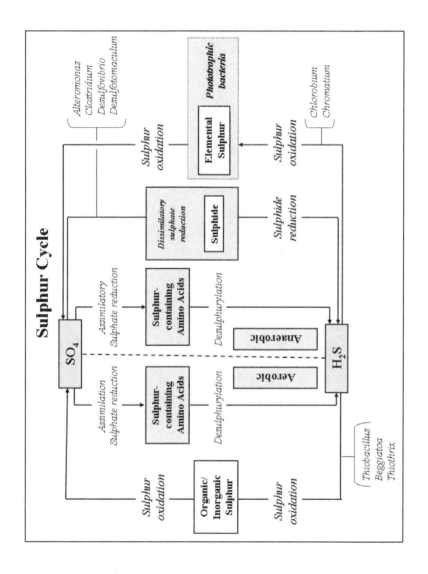

Sulphur Cycle

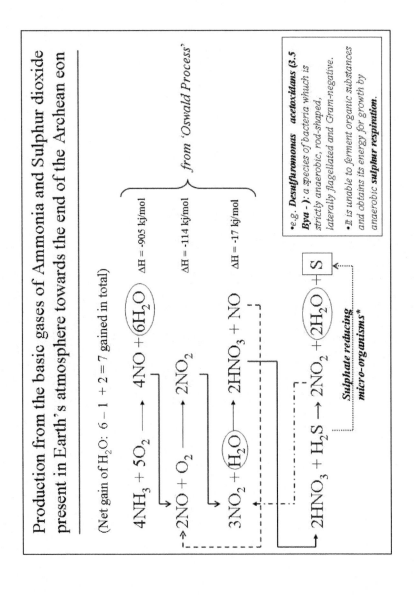

Production from the basic gases of Ammonia and Sulphur dioxide present in Earth's atmosphere towards the end of the Archean eon

(Net gain of H_2O: $6 - 1 + 2 = 7$ gained in total)

$$4NH_3 + 5O_2 \longrightarrow 4NO + 6H_2O \qquad \Delta H = -905 \text{ kj/mol}$$

$$\rightarrow 2NO + O_2 \longrightarrow 2NO_2 \qquad \Delta H = -114 \text{ kj/mol}$$

$$3NO_2 + H_2O \rightarrow 2HNO_3 + NO \qquad \Delta H = -17 \text{ kj/mol}$$

from 'Oswald Process'

$$2HNO_3 + H_2S \rightarrow 2NO_2 + 2H_2O + S$$

*Sulphate reducing micro-organisms**

•e.g. *Desulfuromonas acetoxidans (3.5 Bya -)*: a species of bacteria whuch is strictly anaerobic, rod-shaped, laterally flagellated and Gram-negative.
•It is unable to ferment organic substances and obtains its energy for growth by anaerobic *sulphur respiration*.

Anoxic Waters

Anoxic waters are areas of water that are depleted of dissolved oxygen and are generally of high salinity.

Anoxic conditions will occur if the rate of oxidation of organic matter by bacteria is greater than the supply of dissolved oxygen.

When oxygen is depleted in water, bacteria first turn to the second-best electron acceptor (which in sea water) is nitrate. Denitrification occurs, and the nitrate will be consumed rather rapidly. After reducing some other minor elements, the bacteria will turn to reducing sulphate.

This results in the byproduct of hydrogen sulphide (H_2S), a chemical toxic to most biota.

$$2CH_2O + SO^{2-}_4 \rightarrow 2HCO^-_3 + H_2S + \textbf{chemical energy}$$

Some *chemolithotrophs* can also facilitate the oxidation of hydrogen sulfide into elemental sulphur, according to the following chemical equation:

$$H_2S + O_2 \rightarrow S + H_2O_2$$

Gradual environmental changes through *eutrophication* or **global warming** can cause major oxic-anoxic regime shifts. Based on model studies this can occur abruptly, with a transition between an oxic state dominated by *cyanobacteria*, and an anoxic state with sulphate-reducing bacteria and phototrophic sulphur bacteria.

(See Sulphur Cycle)

Anoxic Coastland Waters

(2021)

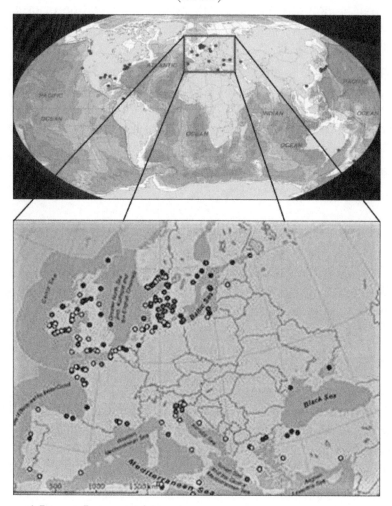

ref: European Environmental Agency

Will Oceans run out of Oxygen by 2030?

Around the globe, the effects of climate cannot be ignored. The world is facing some of the biggest environmental challenges the present generations have ever seen. The impact of the climate includes severe heat waves, rising seas, increased insect outbreaks. It is even possible the oxygen may be drained out of the world's oceans. The loss of ocean oxygen is scary. What will happen to humanity if the world's oceans are dead?

A new study reveals that deoxygenation or a drop in the amount of oxygen dissolved in the oceans due to climate change is already detected in some parts of the world. However, widespread loss of ocean oxygen will be even more evident across large parts of the ocean between 2030 and 2040. The research team, led by climate scientist Dr. Matthew Long, one of the climate scientists at the **National Centre for Atmospheric Research (NCAR)**, found that deoxygenation caused by climate change could already be detected in the Atlantic basins, southern Indian Ocean and parts of the eastern tropical Pacific. And the bad news is, more widespread detection of deoxygenation caused by climate change is possible between 2030 and 2040. Scientists have asserted that a warming climate can gradually drain oceans of oxygen, endangering marine life.

Dr. Long, said *"loss of oxygen in the ocean is one of the serious impacts of a warming atmosphere, and is a major threat to marine life. It is a known fact that warm waters may result in less oxygen absorption. In warm water, the oxygen that is absorbed has a more difficult time going deeper into the ocean. The scientists explained that as water heats up, it expands, becoming lighter than the water below it and is less likely to sink. Although there is evidence that deoxygenation of the ocean was caused by warming climate, it is not enough to conclude that climate change is the main culprit of the oxygen drain. The study pointed out that in some parts of the ocean, including areas off the east coasts of Africa, Australia, and Southeast Asia, deoxygenation caused by climate change may not be evident even by 2100.*

There is an important factor to consider. One is the natural variability of oxygen concentrations in the world's oceans".

In addition, Dr. Long said *"The flow of oxygen in the ocean is interesting and complex. The ocean gets its oxygen supply from the surface from the atmosphere or from phytoplankton, which release oxygen into the water through photosynthesis. Interestingly, natural warming and cooling is attributed to constantly changing oxygen concentrations at the sea surface. These changes can linger for years or even decades deeper in the ocean. This means cold water would allow the ocean surface to absorb a large amount of oxygen, then flow deeper. The oxygen may then stay in the deep of the ocean for years. In contrast, hot weather could lead to natural 'dead zones' in the ocean. This is where fish, crabs, and other marine life cannot survive".*

Mina Fabulous   Wed May 4, 2016

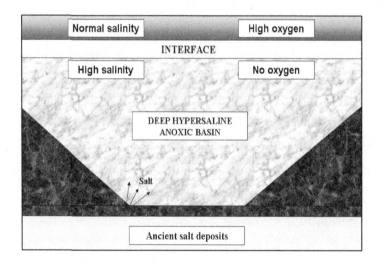

Evolution of the Universe's Future

The **second law of thermodynamics** determines whether a physical or chemical process is forbidden or may occur spontaneously.

Planck stated the second law as follows.

> *'Every process occurring in nature proceeds in the sense in which the sum of the entropies of all bodies taking part in the process is increased.'*

No energy is provided by the surroundings and the second law requires that the entropy of the system alone must therefore increase: $\Delta S > 0$.

All projections of the future of Earth, the Solar System, and the Universe must therefore take account of *entropy*.

More simply stated: *'entropy, or a loss of the energy available to do work, must rise over time'*.

Stars will inevitably exhaust their supply of hydrogen fuel and burn out. Within the Solar System, the Sun will likely expand sufficiently to overwhelm many of the inner planets, Mercury, Venus and Earth, but not the giant planets including Jupiter and Saturn.

Afterwards, the Sun would be reduced to the size of a **white dwarf**, and the outer planets and their moons would continue orbiting this diminutive solar remnant.

However, as gravity is the most important force operating on cosmological scales, it may be difficult or impossible to apply the second law to the universe as a whole.

Physicists do expect though that matter itself will eventually come under the influence of **radioactive decay**, as even the most stable materials break apart into subatomic particles.

If there is just enough matter in the Universe for its gravitational force to bring the expansion associated with the Big Bang to a stop in an infinitely long time, the Universe is said to be 'flat'.

Present data would indicate that the Universe has very close to a 'flat geometry' and therefore will not collapse in on itself after a finite time.

The infinite future allows for the occurrence of a number of massively improbable events, even giving possible rebirth to yet another generation Universe.

10,000 years from now
Random Mating
If globalization trends lead to *panmixia*, human genetic variation will no longer be regionalized. The effective population size, or the **number of breeding individuals in the population**, will tend towards equating to the **actual population size**.

100,000 years from now
Terraforming
Time required to terraform Mars with an oxygen-rich breathable atmosphere, using only plants with solar efficiency comparable to the biosphere currently found on Earth.

100,000 – 1 Million years from now
Colonization occurs
Estimated time by which humanity could colonize the Milky Way galaxy and become capable of harnessing all the energy of the galaxy.

(see 'Kardashev Scale' P703)

1 Million years from now
The Sun's New Rival

Betelgeuse, also known as *Alpha Orionis*, is located in the constellation Orion, and it is one of the biggest and brightest stars in the galactic neighbourhood. It could swallow the Sun twenty times over and emits over 100,000 times more light.

The star is nearing the end of its lifespan and it is estimated that Betelgeuse could go supernova any time within the next million years. It would take 640 years of travelling through the interstellar medium before the light made its way to Earth. That means Betelgeuse could have already exploded hundreds of years ago, and there is no way of knowing.

When that light does arrive, the intensity of the supernova as seen here on Earth may well be able to be seen during the daytime and will outshine the Moon at night.

1.4 Million years in the Future
Turbulent Times

A rogue star could seriously upset the icy comets in the Oort cloud. The star, tentatively known as **Gliese 710**, is an orange dwarf currently located some 63.8 light-years from Earth in Serpens constellation. This star is expected to pass near the Solar System in about 1.35 million years. At its closest, light emanating from Gliese 710 will take 77 days to reach Earth.

It is calculated that the star will pass at a distance of 13,365 AU of Earth's sun. While not exactly close at 1.2 million miles, in cosmological terms the distance is close enough for **Gliese 710** to draw in its gravitational force comets from the Solar System's Oort cloud,

Researchers have now located over 100,000 stars, a massive 156 of which need to be monitored very closely as they might some day pose an imminent threat to humanity.

2 Million years from now
Multiple of Human Species

Vertebrate species separated for this long will generally undergo *allopatric speciation.*

If humanity has been dispersed among genetically isolated space colonies over this time, the galaxy will host an evolutionary radiation of multiple human species with a 'diversity of form and adaptation that would astound us'. This would be a natural process of isolated populations, unrelated to potential deliberate genetic enhancement technologies.

50 Million years from now
Death of Phobos

Located 9,375 kilometres from the centre of Mars and about 6,000 kilometres above the planet's surface is Phobos, one of Mars' two natural satellites. This moon orbits its parent planet from a distance shorter than that of any other known moon in the Solar System.

Because of the short distance from Mars, Phobos completes one full orbit around the planet before it can make one full rotation around its axis.

A combination of the rather short orbital period of the small moon, its close proximity to the planet, and *gravitational tidal interactions* between Phobos and Mars is causing the orbital radius to decrease even further, which will eventually give way to one of two things. Either Phobos will break apart and form an intricate set of rings that could rival the ones that famously belong to Saturn, or Phobos will reach Mars' *Roche Limit*, a region estimated to lie around 5,700 kilometres above the Martian surface, at which point tidal forces will start to pull Phobos apart and it will crash into the surface of Mars, acting as a gigantic nuclear bomb.

100 Million years from now
Technological Civilizations at their limit?
Maximal estimated lifespan of technological civilizations according to Nikolai Kardashev's Civilization Scale later amended by Frank Drake's equation.

1Billion years from now
Migration Rules OK
Estimated time for an astro-engineering project to alter the Earth's orbit, compensating for the Sun's rising brightness and outward migration of the habitable zone, accomplished by repeated asteroid gravity assists.

"We on Earth marvel, and rightfully so, at the daily return of our single Sun. But from a planet orbiting a star in a distant globular cluster, a still more glorious dawn awaits. Not a sunrise, but a galaxy rise. A morning filled with 400 billion suns, the rising of the Milky Way."

Carl Sagan

The Kardashev Scale

In 1964, Russian astrophysicist **Nikolai Kardashev** figured that civilizations could be categorized by the total amount of energy available to them. He defined three levels of civilizations based on their capacity to harness and use power These have since been expanded by another four.

The **Kardashev Scale** is a method of measuring a civilization's level of technological advancement, based on the amount of energy a civilization is able to use for communication, proposed by **Nikolai Kardashev.**

The **Kardashev's civilization rating** is suggested by **Carl Sagan** from the **Kardashev's scale.**

$$K = \frac{log_{10}P - 6}{10}$$

where value K is a civilization's Kardashev rating and   P is the power it uses, in watts.

Type 0

A civilization that harnesses the energy of its home planet, but not to its full potential just yet.

Earth is currently at about 0.73 on the Kardashev Scale. It is presumed that type I will be reached in about 100 years, depending on how fast technology advances.

Type I

A civilization that is capable of harnessing the total energy of its home planet.

Type II

An interstellar civilization, capable of harnessing the total energy output of a star.

Type III

A galactic civilization, capable of inhabiting and harnessing the energy of an entire galaxy

Type IV

A universal civilization, capable of harnessing the energy of the whole universe.

Type V

A multiverse culture, capable of harnessing the energy of multiple universes.

Type VI

A multiverse culture that exists *outside* of time and space, and is capable of creating universes and multiverses and destroying them just as easily.

The **Kardashev's civilization rating** is suggested by **Carl Sagan** from the **Kardashev's scale**.

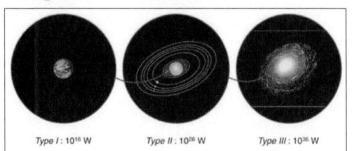

Type I : 10^{16} W   Type II : 10^{26} W   Type III : 10^{36} W

Estimation of energy consumption in the three types of civilizations defined in the Kardashev scale
(Photo Credit : Indif / Wikimedia Commons)

Carl Sagan suggested defining intermediate values (not considered in Kardashev's original scale) by interpolating and extrapolating the values given above for types I (1016 W), II (1026 W) and III (1036 W), which would produce the formula.

4 Billion years in the Future
Our Solar System Dies

 Long before the Sun dies, the Earth will be gone, possibly swallowed up by the Sun as it transitions from a **main sequence** star to a **red giant**.

Before those events occur, all of the water on the planet will evaporate, the rolling hills of green will wither away, and the atmosphere will be lost permanently to space, taking away life and any remaining semblance of the features that are so much a part of Earth.

If the surviving outer planets are not forced into wider orbits around the dying Sun, they might be flung from the Solar System entirely. After that, some of the icy moons might see a glimmer of spring for the first time, allowing a small window of time to pass during which they thaw out and potentially become habitable.

5 Billion years in the Future

Soon afterwards, the Andromeda galaxy will collide with our Milky Way, forming a large elliptical galaxy.

The Solar System can currently be found in the Orion spur of one of our galaxy's spiral arms, situated some 25,000 light-years back from the central core, but after the merger, it is expected to be pushed back to about 100,000 light-years from the centre of the galaxy.

The central region of the newly-formed super galaxy will go through a drastic phase change of its own. The merger will inevitably result in super-massive black holes from both galaxies combining to form an ultra-massive black hole with the combined mass of billions of suns.

Throughout the gradual process of this merger, which will take place over the course of hundreds of millions of years, it is unlikely that any two stars or planets will collide.

The distance separating each individual star is incomprehensibly vast. Even the regions that are densely packed, like globular clusters and nebular clouds, are very spacious.

However, along with absorbing all of the stars, planets, and black holes of Andromeda, the cache of the raw materials for star formation will combine, triggering the birth of hundreds of millions of new stars.

Chance of a stellar collision

Our Sun is about 696.600km in radius. A golf-ball is about 2.14cm in radius. So that gives us a scale of 1cm to 325.500km (rounded).

The nearest star to our Sun is Proxima Centauri (Alpha Centauri C) which is about 39.9 trillion kilometres.

Therefore:

$$1 \text{cm}/(3.255 \times 10^5 \text{km}) \times (3.99 \times 10^{13} \text{km}) = 1.22 \times 10^8 \text{cm}$$

That is too large a number to keep in centimetres, so let us convert that to kilometres, so 1.220 km or 760 miles to the nearest star to the Sun. On the same scale, Proxima Centauri will be about the size of a pea!

This means that this is like placing a golf-ball on the top of the Empire State Building in New York and a pea on the top of the Willis Tower in Chicago (plenty of nothingness in between - and you would still have 40 miles to spare!).

So while we are talking in terms of 400 billion stars in the Milky Way and 1.000 billion in the Andromeda galaxy, the chance of eventual stellar collisions when the two galaxies 'collide' in the future is fairly remote.

10 Billion years in the Future
The Dust Settles

After the merger is complete, the dust will finish settling, leaving behind scant evidence to suggest an epic merger took place at all. However, by observing white dwarfs and calculating their age, and their concentration of heavy metals, future astronomers may be able to deduce the existence of an event that triggered furious star formation.

After an uncertain number of years, new star formation will halt altogether in this newly formed elliptical galaxy. Once the last remaining evidence of material for star formation is gone, a galaxy almost entirely devoid of gas and dust will remain.

Some of the material will be recycled when the first generation of stars produced in the new super-galaxy produced jointly by the Milky Way and Andromeda galaxies explode as brilliant supernovae blasts.

Moreover, some of the most famous far-off nebulae will also be gone. There will be no Orion nebula, no VY Canis Majoris, and no Pillars of Creation. But perhaps the new galaxy will construct even more elaborate nebulae in the wake of all those lost to time.

100 Billion years in the Future
The light starts to dim

100 billion years from now, the ever-accelerating expansion of the universe, most commonly called *dark energy*, will cause all but a few members of the Virgo super-cluster – where the Milky Way galaxy, along with other members of the local group, reside – to *red-shift* into oblivion, never to be seen again by astronomers in our galaxy or any other.

The visibility of galaxies located on the horizon of the observable universe at this point can be likened to light that is captured by the *event horizon* of a *black hole*.

It is much too far away and is travelling way too fast to ever reach our corner of the universe, no matter how much time the light has to traverse spacetime.

In a similar frame of mind, this period signals the regression of the universe. Instead of being diverse, colourful, and bright, as it is now, it devolves into the universe it once was long before Earth was even around ... the cosmic dark ages.

1 Trillion years in the Future
Goodbye forever to Cosmic Microwave Background Radiation

In a trillion years, evidence of the Big Bang in the form of the **cosmic microwave background radiation**, which was created a mere 379,000 years after the birth of the Universe, will grow dim to the point of invisibility. From there, it will then be lost forever.

However, future generations may eventually discover the process of *nucleosynthesis* in the core of red dwarf stars, which are smaller, dimmer, cooler, and much more common than stars like the Sun. They employ an internal process that allows them to burn for trillions of years.

Due to a number of obstacles, one of which is the dwindling supply of star formation materials, the production of stars will ultimately halt, leaving behind nothing but red dwarf stars.

There will be no more supernova blasts to use as *standard candles*, no more food to quench the insatiable appetite of *black holes*, no new planets, and no more cosmic nebulae.

100 Trillion years in the Future
The Universe Dies

A number of hypotheses that predict how the universe will end have been floated, but the most promising one is called '**the big chill**'.

Under this scenario, *dark energy* continues driving the expansion of the universe, resulting in temperatures dropping throughout the universe until it reaches a minute fraction of a degree above absolute zero.

Similarly, if the expansion of the universe continues, planets, stars, and galaxies will eventually be pulled so far apart that stars will lose access to the raw material needed for star formation, and thus the lights will inevitably go out for good.

Glossary

Absorption lines: By measuring the location of lines in astronomical spectra, astronomers can determine the red shift of the receding sources.

Acellular: Life that exists without a cellular structure for at least part of its life cycle.

Accretion: The coming together and cohesion of matter under the influence of gravitation to form larger bodies.

Acritarchs: Organic microfossils, known from approximately 1,800 million years ago.

Actin: A protein that forms (together with myosin) the contractile filaments of muscle cells, and is also involved in motion in other types of cell.

Adenosine Triphosphate: (ATP) An organic compound that provides energy to drive many processes in living cells.

Aerosols: Minute particles suspended in the atmosphere. Dispersal of volcanic aerosols has a drastic effect on Earth's climate.

Agnathan: A group of primitive jawless vertebrates which includes the lampreys, hagfishes, and many fossil fish-like forms.

Albedo Effect: When applied to the Earth is a measure of how much of the Sun's energy is reflected back into space. Overall, the Earth's albedo has a cooling effect.

Algal Reef: An organic reef which has been formed largely of algal remains and in which algae are or were the main lime-secreting organisms.

Allantois: The foetal membrane lying below the *chorion* in many vertebrates, formed as an outgrowth of the embryo's gut. In birds and reptiles it grows to surround the embryo.

Allopatric speciation: Speciation that happens when two populations of the same species become isolated from each other due to geographic changes.

Alvarez Hypothesis: An hypothesis which posits that the mass extinction of the non-avian dinosaurs and many other living things during the Cretaceous–Paleogene extinction event was caused by the impact of a large asteroid on the Earth.

Amiote: An animal whose embryo develops in an *amnion* and *chorion* and has an *allantois*; a mammal, bird, or reptile.

Amnion: The innermost membrane that encloses the embryo of a mammal, bird, or reptile.

Amniotic Egg: An evolutionary invention that allowed the first reptiles to colonize dry land more than 300 million years ago.

Ampullae of Lorenzini: Electroreceptors, sense organs able to detect electric fields. They form a network of mucus-filled pores in the skin of cartilaginous fish. They evolved from the mechanosensory organs of early vertebrates. Most bony fishes and terrestrial vertebrates have lost their Ampullae of Lorenzini.

Anaerobic: Relating to or requiring an absence of free oxygen.

Anapsid: An *amniote* whose skull lacks one or more skull openings (*fenestra*, or *fossae*) near the temples.

Anerobes: A micro-organism that is able to, or can only, live in the absence of oxygen.

Anthropic: Involving or concerning the existence of human life, especially as a constraint on theories of the universe.

Annulated: Having rings; marked with or formed of rings.

Anoxic Event: Period when large expanses of Earth's oceans are depleted of dissolved oxygen (O_2), creating toxic and euxinic waters.

Anthropic: Involving or concerning the existence of human life, especially as a constraint on theories of the universe

Anthropocene: The current geological age, viewed as the period during which human activity has been the dominant influence on climate and the environment.

Apex predator: Usually defined in terms of trophic dynamics, meaning that they occupy the highest trophic levels.

Arboreal: Inhabiting or frequenting trees.

Archaic: Characteristic of an earlier or more primitive time.

Archean: Relating to or denoting the eon that constitutes the earlier (or middle) part of the Precambrian, in which there was no life on the Earth.

Archosaur: Extinct archosaurs include non-avian *dinosaurs*, *pterosaurs*, and extinct relatives of *crocodilians*.

Arroyo: A dry creek, stream bed or gulch that temporarily or seasonally fills and flows after sufficient rain.

Arthropoda: Invertebrates with segmented bodies and jointed limbs. The exoskeleton or cuticles consists of chitin.

Asthenosphere: The upper layer of the Earth's mantle, below the lithosphere.

Astraspidiform: A small group of extinct armoured jawless vertebrates.

Astrobleme: An eroded remnant of a large crater made by the impact of a meteorite or comet.

Astronomical Unit (AU):   A unit of length, roughly the distance from Earth to the Sun and equal to 150 million kilometres or 8.3 light minutes.

Atrophied: Having lost effectiveness or vigour due to under use or neglect.

Australopithecine: A fossil bipedal primate with both ape-like and human characteristics, found in Pliocene and Lower Pleistocene deposits (circa 4 million to 1 million years old) in Africa.

Avialan: Any animal belonging to the clade Avialae, including all birds and some dinosaurian relatives.

Axon: A bundle of fibres that uses electrical and chemical signals to transmit sensory and motor information from one body part to another.

Bacillus: A rod-shaped bacterium causing disease.

Baculitidae: A family of extinct ammonoids that lived mostly during the Late Cretaceous.

Basal: Forming or belonging to a bottom layer or base.

Benthic: The collection of organisms living on or in the bottom of a body of water.

Benthopelagic: Relating to species living at the bottom of the sea.

Bifid Claw: A claw which is divided by a deep cleft or notch into two parts.

Bilaterian: An animal having bilateral symmetry. Animals, including humans, with this two-sided symmetry are referred to as being bilaterians.

Black Hole: A region of space having a gravitational field so intense that no matter or radiation can escape.

refer **Bony Fish**: *Osteichthyes*, popularly red to as the bony fish, is a diverse taxonomic group of fish that have skeletons primarily composed of bone tissue. They can be contrasted with the *Chondrichthyes*, which have skeletons primarily composed of cartilage.

Brane: An extended object analogous to the strings of string theory, but having any number of dimensions rather than one dimension.

Brumate: To be in a lethargic state, somewhat analogous to hibernation but not the same. Commonly found in reptiles and in some other animal species.

Buccal Cavity: Relating to the mouth. It has the same meaning as oral. In the context of anatomy, a cavity is a hollow spot inside the body.

Caecum: A pouch connected to the junction of the small and large intestines.

Calcareous: Containing calcium carbonate; chalky.

Capitate: Ending in a distinct compact head.

Carotenoids: Naturally occurring pigments found in plants.

Carpace: The hard upper shell of a tortoise, crustacean, or arachnid.

Cartilaginous: *Chondrichthyes* is a class of jawed fishes having a cartilaginous skeleton. The class includes a diverse group of fishes including sharks, rays, skates and chimaeras. They are mostly marine fishes. The other group of fishes are bony fishes, which are included in the class *Osteichthyes*.

Caudal: At or near the tail or the posterior part of the body.

Centripetal Force: A force that acts on a body moving in a circular path and is directed towards the centre around which the body is moving.

Cephalization: The concentration of sense organs, nervous control, etc., at the anterior end of the body, forming a head and brain, both during evolution and in the course of an embryo's development.

Cephalon: In some *arthropods*, especially *trilobites*, the region of the head composed of fused segments.

Cephalopods: An active predatory mollusc of the large class *Cephalopoda*, such as an octopus or squid.

Chelae: Each of a pair of hinged pincer-like claws terminating the anterior limbs of a crab, lobster, or scorpion, typically curved and sharply pointed and used for feeding, defence, and courtship. Compare with **chelicerae**.

Chelicerae: Either of a pair of appendages in front of the mouth in arachnids and some other arthropods usually modified as pincer-like claws. Compare with **chelae**.

Chimaeras: Any of a family (*Chimaeridae*) of marine cartilaginous fishes with a tapering or threadlike tail and usually no anal fin.

Chironomid: An insect of a family *Chironomidae* that comprises the non-biting midges.

Chloroplasts: In green plant cells which contains chlorophyll and in which photosynthesis takes place.

Choana: Posterior nasal apertures or internal nostrils. They are two openings found at the back of the nasal passage between the nasal cavity and the throat in tetrapods, including humans and other mammals.

Chordates: An animal of the large phylum *Chordata*, comprising the vertebrates together with the *sea squirts* and *lancelets*.

Chorion: The outermost membrane surrounding an embryo of a reptile, bird, or mammal. In mammals it contributes to the formation of the placenta.

Chromophore: The part of a molecule responsible for its colour. The colour that is seen by our eyes is the one not absorbed by the reflecting object within a certain wavelength spectrum of visible light.

Chronospecies: Defined as a single lineage whose morphology changes with time. At some point, it is judged that enough change has occurred that two forms, separated in time and anatomy, once existed.

Cicada: A large *homopterous* insect with long transparent wings, found chiefly in warm countries. The male *cicada* makes a loud, shrill droning noise by vibrating two membranes on its abdomen.

Cilia: A short microscopic hair-like vibrating structure found in large numbers on the surface of certain cells, either causing currents in the surrounding fluid, or, in some *protozoans* and other small organisms, providing propulsion.

Circadian Rhythm: Essentially a 24-hour cycle that runs in the background of the brain, and cycles between sleepiness and alertness at regular intervals to carry out essential functions and processes.

Clade: A group of organisms that are composed of a 'common ancestor' and all its lineal descendants.

Cladistics: A method of classification of animals and plants. It aims to identify and take account of only those shared characteristics which can be deduced to have originated in the common ancestor of a group of species during evolution, not those arising by convergence.

Cloacae: A common cavity at the end of the digestive tract for the release of both excretory and genital products in vertebrates (except most mammals) and certain invertebrates.

Coacervate: A colloid-rich viscous liquid phase that may separate from a colloidal solution on addition of a third component.

Coccus: Any spherical or roughly spherical bacterium.

Columbia: About 1.6 billion years ago Columbia, also known as Nuna or Hudsonland, was one of Earth's ancient supercontinents.

Continental Drift: Hypothesis that the Earth's continents have moved over geologic time relative to each other, thus appearing to have 'drifted' across the ocean bed.

Cornea: The transparent front part of the eye that covers the iris, pupil, and ommatidium when these and others are present.

Corus arteriosus: Also known as *infundibulum*, the *conus arteriosus* is a conical pouch formed from the upper and left angle of the right ventricle in the chordate heart, from which the pulmonary trunk arises.

Cosmine: A spongy, bony material that makes up the dentine-like layers in the scales of the lobe-finned fishes of the class *Sarcopterygii*.

Cosmoid: Fish scales that include layers of cosmine are known as cosmoid scales.

Craniate: An animal that possesses a skull.

Crinoids: An *echinoderm* of the class *Crinoidea*, which comprises the sea lilies and feather stars.

Crown Group: A living monophyletic group, or clade, consisting of the last common ancestor of all living examples, plus all of its descendants.

Cryptobiosis: A metabolic state of life entered by an organism in response to adverse environmental conditions such as desiccation, freezing, and oxygen deficiency.

Ctenoid: Scales that have a variously developed spiny posterior margin.

Ctenii: Spinules or teeth on the posterior margin of a ctenoid scale.

Cultrate: Sharp-edged and pointed; knifelike

Cuticula: A *cuticula*, or cuticle, is any of a variety of tough but flexible, non-mineral outer coverings of an organism, or parts of an organism, that provide protection.

Cycloid: Scales have a smooth posterior margin lacking *ctenii*.

Dark Energy: A theoretical form of energy postulated to act in opposition to gravity and to occupy the entire universe, accounting for most of the energy in it and causing its expansion to accelerate.
Einstein's theories allow for the possible existence of dark energy.

Deccan Traps: A large igneous province of west-central India. It is one of the largest volcanic features on Earth, taking the form of a large shield volcano. It consists of numerous layers of solidified flood basalt that together are more than about 2,000m thick, cover an area of about 500,000 square kilometres, and have a volume of about 1,000,000 cubic kilometres.

Dentine: Hard dense bony tissue forming the bulk of a tooth, beneath the enamel.

Dermal: Of or relating to the skin.

De Sitter Universe: Models the Universe as spatially flat and neglects ordinary matter, so the dynamics of the Universe are dominated by the cosmological constant, thought to correspond to 'dark energy' in our Universe or the 'inflation field' in the early Universe.

Detritivores: Animals which feed on dead organic material, especially plant detritus.

Detritus: Typically includes the bodies or fragments of bodies of dead organisms, and fecal material

Deuterostome: An animals typically characterized by its anus forming before its mouth during embryonic development. Some examples of *deuterostomes* include vertebrates (and thus humans), sea stars, and *crinoids*. In **deuterostomy**, the developing embryo's first opening (the *blastopore*) becomes the anus, while the mouth is formed at a different site later on.

Dewclaw: A digit – vestigial in some animals – on the foot of many mammals, birds, and reptiles (including some extinct orders, like certain *theropods*).

Dimorphic: Occurring in or representing two distinct forms.

Dinosauromorph: A clade of *avemetatarsalian archosaurs* (reptiles closer to birds than to *crocodilians*) that includes the *Dinosauria* (dinosaurs) and some of their close relatives.

Doublet structure: In optics, a doublet is a type of lens made up of two simple lenses paired together.

Ductus arteriosus: A normal foetal artery connecting the main body artery (aorta) and the main lung artery (pulmonary artery). The ductus allows blood to detour away from the lungs before birth. Every baby is born with a *ductus arteriosus*.

Ecdysis: The process of shedding the old skin (in reptiles) or casting off the outer cuticle (in insects and other arthropods).

Echinoderm: A marine invertebrate of the phylum *Echinodermata*, such as a starfish, sea urchin, or sea cucumber.

Ectodermal: The outermost layer of cells or tissue of an embryo in early development, or the parts derived from this.

Ejecta: Material that is forced or thrown out, especially as a result of volcanic eruption, meteoritic impact, or stellar explosion.

Endospore: A resistant asexual spore that develops inside some bacteria cells.

Endothermic: An animal dependent on or capable of the internal generation of heat.

Eponymous: Named after a particular person or group.

Estivate: To spend a hot or dry period in a prolonged state of torpor or dormancy.

Eugeneodont: The meaning of the name Eugeneodont correlates to 'true origin teeth', and comes from the Greek **eu** (good/true), **geneos** (race, kind, origin), and **odon** (tooth). The *Eugeneodontida* disappeared in the Early Triassic.

Eukaryotes: Organisms whose bodies are made up of eukaryotic cells, such **as** protists, fungi, plants and animals. Eukaryotic cells are cells that contain a nucleus and organelles, and are enclosed by a plasma membrane.

Euxinic: Having a high concentration of hydrogen sulphide and no oxygen.

Event Horizon: As an object approaches the 'point of no return' of a Black Hole, its image appears to freeze and fade away because you cannot see any of the light it emits from that point forward.

Evertible: Capable of being inverted or subjected to inversion.

Exaptation: 'Exaptation' and the related term 'co-option' describe a shift in the function of a trait during evolution. For example, a trait can evolve because it served one particular function, but subsequently it may come to serve another.

Extremophile: A microorganism, especially an archaean, that lives in conditions of extreme temperature, acidity, alkalinity, or chemical concentration.

Eyespots: Photoreceptive organelles found in the flagellate or (motile) cells of green algae and other unicellular photosynthetic organisms such as *euglenids*. They allow the cells to sense light direction and intensity and respond to them, prompting the organisms to either swim towards the light or away from it.

Fimbriae: Small, finger-like projections at the end of the fallopian tubes, through which eggs move from the ovaries to the uterus.

Flagella: Flagella are commonly found in bacteria, but can also be found in *archaea* and *eukaryotic* organisms as well. A flagellum is a lash-like structure that protrudes from the cell body.

Flame cell: A specialized excretory cell found in the simplest freshwater invertebrates, including flatworms, rotifers and *nemerteans*. These are the simplest animals to have a dedicated excretory system. Flame cells function like a kidney, removing waste materials.

Flicker Fusion Rate: The frequency at which an intermittent light stimulus appears to be completely steady.

Foraminifera: Single-celled organisms, members of a phylum or class of *amoeboid protists* characterized by streaming granular ectoplasm for catching food and other uses.

Friedmann expansion: The idea of an evolving universe that contained moving matter.

Ga: Gigaannum or one billion years.

Ganoid: Relating to or being a kind of fish scale that is hard and bony with a shiny surface composed of an enamel-like substance.

Gastroliths: Small stones swallowed by a bird, reptile, or fish to aid digestion in the gizzard.

Glabella: The smooth part of the forehead above and between the eyebrows.

Gluons: Elementary particles that act as 'exchange particles' (or gauge bosons) for the strong force between quarks.

Gondwana: A large landmass often referred to as a supercontinent that formed during the late Neoproterozoic and began to break up during the Jurassic.

Gracile: Having a light, thin body. Used especially in anthropology to describe modern types of human.

Gram negative: Bacteria that have a **thin** *peptidoglycan* layer and **have** an outer lipid membrane.

Gram positive: Bacteria that have a **thick** *peptidoglycan* layer and **no** outer lipid membrane.

Granitoids: A generic term for a diverse category of coarse-grained igneous rocks that consist predominantly of quartz, plagioclase, and alkali feldspar.

Great Dying: The biggest extinction the planet has ever experienced. Happened some 250 million years ago at the time of the Permian-Triassic extinction and was largely caused by greenhouse gases in the atmosphere.

GUT: A **Grand Unified Theory** is a model in particle physics in which, at high energies, the three gauge interactions of the Standard Model comprising the electromagnetic, weak, and strong forces are merged into a single force.

Hadean: A geologic eon preceding the Archean. It began with the formation of the Earth about 4.6 billion years ago.

Halophile: An organism, especially a microorganism, that grows in or can tolerate saline conditions.

Harderian gland: A gland found within the eye's orbit and that occurs in *tetrapods* which possess a nictitating membrane.

Hemibranchs: A gill having lamellae or filaments only on one side.

Hertzprung-Russell: A scatter plot of stars showing the relationship between absolute magnitudes or luminosities versus stellar classifications or effective temperatures.

Heterodont: A set of teeth of various shapes that may serve different functions (e.g. incisors, canines, and molars).

Heterotroph: An organism deriving its nutritional requirements from complex organic substances.

Hipparcos: A scientific satellite of the European Space Agency launched in 1989 and operated until 1993. It was the first space experiment devoted to accurate measurement of the positions of celestial objects on the sky and aimed to collect data centring on an object's speed, velocity, and trajectory.

Holotype: A single type specimen upon which the description and name of a new species is based.

Hominid: A primate of a family *Hominidae* which includes humans and their fossil ancestors, and also (in recent schemes) at least some of the great apes.

Hominini: A primate of a taxonomic tribe (*Hominini*), which comprises those species regarded as human, directly ancestral to humans, or very closely related to humans.

Hominoid: A primate of a group that includes humans, their fossil ancestors, and the anthropoid apes.

Homologous: Similar in position, structure, and evolutionary origin but not necessarily in function.

Humerus: The long bone in the upper arm. It is located between the elbow joint and the shoulder. At the elbow, it connects primarily to the ulna, as the forearm's radial bone connects to the wrist.

Ileum: The third portion of the small intestine, between the jejunum and the caecum.

Impactor: A meteorite impact, occurring when a rocky, metallic (typically iron), or icy body that had been orbiting the Sun passes through the atmosphere to hit the Earth's surface.

Integument: A natural outer covering or coat, such as the skin of an animal or the membrane enclosing an organ.

Kellwasser Event: Event which occurred around the time established by the boundary between the Frasnian and the Famennian stages of late Devonian when 19% of all families and 50% of all genera became extinct.

Kelvin: Although initially defined by the freezing point of water the Celsius scale is now officially a derived scale, defined in relation to the Kelvin temperature scale. Zero on the Celsius scale (0°C) is now defined as equivalent to 273.15K, with a temperature difference of 1^{0}C equivalent to a difference of 1K, meaning the unit size in each scale is the same. This means that 100°C, previously defined as the boiling point of water, is now defined as the equivalent to 373.15K.

Kleptoplasty: A symbiotic phenomenon whereby plastids, notably chloroplasts from algae, are sequestered by host organisms. The word is derived from *kleptes* (κλέπτης), Greek for thief.

Konservat-Lagerstätte: Sites of deposits known for the extraordinary preservation of fossilized life forms, especially where the soft parts are preserved.

Kuiper Belt: A region of the Solar System beyond the orbit of Neptune, believed to contain many comets, asteroids, and other small bodies made largely of ice.

Labyrinthodont: Labyrinthodont (name meaning 'maze-toothed') was a subclass of amphibian which existed from 395 to 120 million years ago. It is ancestral to all terrestrial vertebrates. This was the first amphibious creature to appear in Primeval.

Lacrimial Bone: A small thin bone making up part of the front inner wall of each orbit and providing a groove for the passage of the lacrimal ducts.

Lamella: A thin layer, membrane, or plate of tissue, especially in bone.

Lapetus Ocean: An ocean that existed in the late Neoproterozoic and early Paleozoic eras.

Lectotype: A biological specimen or illustration later selected to serve as definitive type example of a species or subspecies when the original author of the name did not designate a holotype.

Lepidosireniformes: An order of lungfish with a cylindrical body, paired lungs, and nearly filamentous pectoral and pelvic fins.

Leptons: Subatomic particles, such as electrons, muons, or neutrinos, which do not take part in the strong interaction.

Lissamphibian: Any of the living amphibians, of the subclass *Lissamphibia*, including the frog and salamander families.

Lithology: The study of the general physical characteristics of rocks.

Lithosphere: The rigid outer part of the Earth, consisting of the crust and upper mantle.

Lithospheric Plates: Regions of Earth's crust and upper mantle that are fractured into plates that move across a deeper plasticine mantle.

Lobe-finned: A fish of a largely extinct group having fleshy lobed fins, including the probable ancestors of the amphibians. Compare with ray-finned fish.

Lobopodian: The *lobopodians*, members of the informal group *Lobopodia* (from the Greek, meaning 'blunt feet'), are *panarthropods* with stubby legs called *lobopods*.

Local Group: The galaxy group comprising 54 galaxies and which includes the Milky Way. It has a total diameter of roughly 10 million light-years; 9×10^{22} metres and a total mass of the order of 2×10^{12} solar masses.

Metacarpals: Form a transverse arch to which the rigid row of distal carpal bones are fixed.

Metazoan: Any of a group (*Metazoa*) that comprises all animals having the body composed of cells differentiated into tissues and organs and usually a digestive cavity lined with specialized cells.

Methane Clathrate: A solid compound in which a large amount of methane is trapped within a crystal structure of water, forming a solid similar to ice.

Methanogen: A methane-producing bacterium, especially an *Archaean* which reduces carbon dioxide to methane.

Methanogenisis: The production of methane by bacteria or other living organisms.

Microbiome: The microorganisms in a particular environment, including the body or a part of the body. (Replaces old term of 'flora')

Microorganism: A microscopic organism, especially a bacterium, virus, or fungus which may exist in its single-celled form or as a colony of cells.

Microfossils: Fossils that are generally between 0.001mm and 1mm in size, the visual study of which requires the use of light or electron microscopy.

Microvilli: The millions of tiny, hair-fine, finger-like protrusions on the surface cells of *epithelium* which greatly increase the effective surface area so as to facilitate absorption.

Mitochondrion *(pl mitochondria)***:** An organelle found in large numbers in most cells, in which the biochemical processes of respiration and energy production occur. It has a double membrane, the inner part being folded inwards to form layers (*cristae*).

Monogenesis: The theory that humans are all descended from a single pair of ancestors. Also called *monogeny*.

Monoplyletic: A group of organisms descended from a common evolutionary ancestor or ancestral group, especially one not shared with any other group.

Multicellular: Having, made up of, or involving more than one and usually many cells especially of living matter. It is probable that, with a few exceptions, all the cells in a *multicellular* organism have the same genetic information encoded in the chains of nucleotide bases that make up their DNA.

Mya: Million years ago.

Myomeres: Blocks of skeletal muscle tissue arranged in sequence, commonly found in aquatic *chordates*.

Nematocyst: A specialized cell in the tentacles of a jellyfish or other coelenterate, containing a barbed or venomous coiled thread that can be projected in self-defence or to capture prey.

Neocortex: A part of the cerebral cortex concerned with sight and hearing in mammals, regarded as the most recently evolved part of the cortex.

Neural Arch: An arch of bone or cartilage of a vertebra that is situated posterior to a vertebral body.

Neutrinos: A neutral subatomic particle with a mass close to zero and half-integral spin, which rarely reacts with normal matter.

Niche Partitioning: Refers to the process by which natural selection drives competing species into different patterns of resource use or different niches.

Nitrogen Fixation: The chemical processes by which atmospheric nitrogen is assimilated into organic compounds, especially by certain *microorganisms* as part of the nitrogen cycle.

Noetics: A branch of metaphysics concerning the study of the mind as well as intellect. It covers the field of thinking and knowing, as well as mental operations.

Notochord: An embryonic midline structure common to all members of the phylum *Chordata*, providing both mechanical and signalling cues to the developing embryo. In vertebrates, the notochord is replaced by the *vertebral column*, and becomes the cartilaginous substance between vertebrae.

Nucleoid: An irregularly shaped region within the prokaryotic cell that contains all or most of the genetic material.

Nucleosynthesis: The fusion of heavy elements from lighter ones.

Occipital: Relating to or situated in the back of the head.

Occlusion: A blockage or closing of a blood vessel or hollow organ, or the position of the teeth when the jaws are closed.

Ocelli: Unlike compound eyes, *ocelli* do not form a complex image of the environment, but are used to detect movement. Most *arthropods* possess *ocelli*. Some species of *arthropod* do not possess compound eyes and only have *ocelli*.

Odontodes: About 500 million years ago, jawed vertebrates evolved exoskeletal body armours. It is believed that teeth of jawed vertebrates evolved by modifications of the ridges of tubercles on vertebrate body armour. These '*dermal teeth*' were hard structures found on the external surfaces of animals or near internal openings.

Oldowan: The Oldowan was a widespread stone tool archaeological industry in prehistory.

Ommatidium: Each of the optical units under the cornea that make up the compound eye of an insect.

Omnivorous: Feeding on a variety of food of both plant and animal origin.

Onychophoran: A terrestrial invertebrate of the small phylum *Onychophora*, which comprises the velvet worms.

Oort cloud: A spherical cloud of small rocky and icy bodies postulated to orbit the Sun beyond the orbit of Pluto and up to 1.5 light years from the Sun, and to act as a reservoir of comets.

Operculum: The covering of the gills of a fish.

Opsin: A group of proteins made light-sensitive via the *chromophore retinal* found in photoreceptor cells of the retina.

Ornithischian: Relating to or denoting herbivorous dinosaurs of an order distinguished by having a pelvic structure resembling that of birds. Compare with Saurischian.

Ortholog: A homologous gene that is related to those in different organisms by descent from the DNA of a 'common ancestor'.

Osmolyte: An *organic solute* that helps cells adapt to dehydration or fluid excess. Osmolytes are generated within cells in response to osmotic stresses.

Ossified: Having turned into bone or bony tissue. (refer to Petrified)

Osteichthyes: Popularly referred to as the 'bony fish'.

Ozone Layer: A layer in the Earth's stratosphere at an altitude of about 10km containing a high concentration of ozone, which absorbs most of the ultraviolet radiation reaching the Earth from the Sun.

Pachyostosis: A non-pathological condition in vertebrate animals in which the bones experience a thickening, generally caused by extra layers of lamellar bone.

Paedomorphosis: Phylogenetic change that involves retention of juvenile characters by the adult.

Palatal Fangs: Any sharp teeth occurring on the palate.

Paleo-Tethys Ocean: An ocean located along the northern margin of the paleo-continent Gondwana.

Pangaea Ultima: The hypothesised future supercontinent, Pangaea is a future supercontinent, earning its name due to its similarities with the previous supercontinent, Pangaea.

Panmixia: Random mating within a breeding population.

Panspermia: The theory that life on the earth originated from microorganisms or chemical precursors of life present in outer space and able to initiate life on reaching a suitable environment.

Papilla: A small rounded protuberance on a part or organ of the body.

Pathogenic: Causing or capable of causing disease.

Patrilineal: Relating to or based on relationship to the father or descent through the male line.

Peduncle: A stalk-like part by which an organ is attached to an animal's body, or by which a barnacle or other sedentary animal is attached to a substrate.

Pelagic: Relating to the open sea.

Pelycosaurs: The *pelycosaurs* appear to have been a group of *synapsids* that have direct ancestral links with the mammals, having differentiated teeth and a developing hard palate.

Perfusion: The passage of blood, a blood substitute, or other fluid through the blood vessels or other natural channels in an organ or tissue.

Pericardial cavity: The pericardial cavity contains the heart, the muscular pump that drives the blood around the cardiovascular system.

Periplast: One of three types of cell-covering of three classes of algae.

Peritrichous: Covered all over with uniformly distributed flagella.

Petrified: Organic matter changed into a stony substance. *(refer to Ossified)*

Photon: A type of elementary particle that serves as the quantum of the electromagnetic field, including electromagnetic radiation such as light and radio waves, and the force carrier for the electromagnetic force.

Photosynthetic: Relating to or involved in the process by which green plants, and some other organisms, use sunlight to synthesize nutrients from carbon dioxide and water:

Phototactic: The bodily movement of a motile organism in response to light, either towards the source of light (positive phototaxis) or away from it (negative phototaxis).

Phototroph: An organism that uses energy from sunlight to synthesize organic compounds for nutrition.

Phyllopod Bed: The most famous fossil-bearing member of the Burgess Shale fossil *Lagerstätte*. It was the source of 95% of the fossils collected.

Phylogeny: A branching diagram or a tree showing the evolutionary relationships among various biological species or other entities based upon similarities and differences in their physical or genetic characteristics.

Phylum: A principal taxonomic category that ranks above class and below kingdom.

Picoplankton: The fraction of plankton composed by cells between 0.2 and 2μm that can be either prokaryotic and eukaryotic *phototrophs* and *heterotrophs*. They have an important role in making up a significant portion of the total biomass of phytoplankton communities.

Pineal Gland: From the point of view of biological evolution, the pineal gland is a kind of atrophied photoreceptor. In some species of amphibians and reptiles it is linked to a light-sensing organ, known as the 'parietal eye'.

Piscivorous: A carnivorous animal that eats primarily fish.

Plate Tectonics: A theory explaining the structure of the Earth's crust and many associated phenomena resulting from the interaction of rigid lithospheric plates which move slowly over the underlying mantle.

Plesiomorphic: An evolutionary trait that is homologous within a particular group of organisms, but is not unique to members of that group.

Pollicis longus: This muscle is unique to humans, being either rudimentary or absent in other primates.

Polychaete: A marine annelid worm of the class Polychaeta. A *'Bristle Worm'*.

Posteriad: Towards the posterior part or surface of the body; to the rear of; posteriorly. *Opposed to anteriad.*

Pre-maxilla: One of a pair of small cranial bones at the very tip of the upper jaw of many animals, usually, but not always, bearing teeth.

Primatomorph: A clade of placental mammals containing two orders: *Dermoptera* and *Primates.*

Proboscis: The nose of a mammal, especially when it is long and mobile such as the trunk of an elephant or the snout of a tapir.

Prokaryotic: A microscopic single-celled organism which has neither a distinct nucleus with a membrane nor other specialized organelles, including the *bacteria* and *cyanobacteria*. Compare with *eukaryote*.

Prosimians: Considered to have characteristics that are more 'primitive' (ancestral or plesiomorphic) than those of *simians* (monkeys, apes, and humans).

Prosoma: The fused head and thorax of spiders and other chelicerate arthropods.

Pseudosuchians: One of two major divisions of *Archosauria*, including living *crocodilians* and all *archosaurs* more closely related to *crocodilians* than to birds.

Pterygoid Arches: A paired bone forming part of the palate of many vertebrates.

Pupae: Insects in their inactive immature form between larvae and adults, e.g. Chrysalides.

Pygidium: The terminal part or hind segment of the body in certain invertebrates. In groups other than insects, it contains the *anus* and, in females, the *ovipositor* and is composed of fused body segments.

Pygostyle: In a bird, a triangular plate formed of the fused caudal vertebrae, typically supporting the tail feathers.

Quadrupedalism: Four-footed; using all four feet for walking and running.

Quarks: Any of a number of subatomic particles carrying a fractional electric charge, postulated as building blocks of the hadrons.

Ramus: (*pl rami*) an arm or branch of a bone, in particular those of the ischium and pubes or of the jawbone.

Ray-finned: The ray-finned fishes are so-called because their fins are webs of skin supported by bony or horny spines (rays), Compare with lob-finned fish.

Red Shift: The displacement of spectral lines towards longer wavelengths (the red end of the spectrum) in radiation from distant galaxies and celestial objects.

Rhamphotheca: The horny sheath composed of modified scales of a bird's bill.

Rhipidistian: Also known as *Dipnotetrapodomorpha*, is a clade of lobe-finned fishes which includes the *tetrapods* and lungfishes.

Right Ascension: The distance of a point east of the '*First Point of Aries*', measured along the celestial equator and expressed in hours, minutes, and seconds.

Robust: The variables between populations, and species of hominoids, all of which reflect great variation in the magnitudes of biomechanical loads and the behaviours that produce them.

Radula: An anatomical structure used by mollusks for feeding, sometimes compared to a tongue. It is a minutely toothed, chitinous ribbon, which is typically used for scraping or cutting food before the food enters the oesophagus.

Roche Limit: The distance within which the gravitational field of a large body is strong enough to prevent any smaller body from being held together by gravity.

Rostral: Situated or occurring near the front end of the body, especially in the region of the nose and mouth.

Rugose: Full of wrinkles.

Sagittal Crest: A bony ridge on top of the skull to which chewing muscles attach.

Sanukitoid: A variety of high-Mg *granitoid* found in convergent margin settings.

Saurischian: Relating to or denoting dinosaurs of an order distinguished by having a pelvic structure resembling that of lizards. Compare with Ornithischian.

Scleritic: A medical condition in which body tissue or organs become harder.

Scute: A bony external plate or scale overlaid with horn, as on the shell of a turtle, the skin of *crocodilians*, and the feet of birds.

Selene: Selene was a Titan goddess in Greek mythology, daughter of the Titans Hyperion and Theia. She had two siblings, Helios and Eos.

Septum: *(pl. septa)* A dividing wall, membrane, or the like, in a plant or animal structure.

Sessile: Lacks the ability of self-locomotion and is predominantly immobile. Those animals which are attached to a substrate.

Shatter Cone: A conical fragment of rock that has striations radiating from the apex and that is formed by high pressure (as from volcanism or meteorite impact).

Shocked Quartz: Found worldwide, and occurs in the thin C-Pg boundary layer, which occurs at the contact between Cretaceous and Paleogene rocks. This is further evidence (in addition to iridium enrichment) that the transition between the two geologic periods was caused by a large impact.

Siberian Traps: A large region of volcanic rock, known as a large igneous province in Siberia, Russia. The massive eruptive event that formed the traps is one of the largest known volcanic events in the last 500 million years.

Sink: Any area that absorbs or holds more carbon than it gives off. A carbon sink absorbs carbon dioxide from the atmosphere.

Siphonophores: Colonial *hydrozoans* that reproduce asexually through a budding process.

Speciation: The formation of new biological species as a result of isolation mutation selection. Once two groups are isolated different mutations occur in each group.

Spherules: Tiny glass spherules are created during an impact, generating such intense heat that the crust melts and sprays into the air. The molten material hardens and falls back down as tiny glass beads.

Spiracles: An external respiratory opening, especially each of a number of pores on the body of an insect, or each of a pair of vestigial gill slits behind the eye of a cartilaginous fish.

Spirilla: (*sing, Spirillum*) are a group of bacteria characterized by a corkscrew (spiral) appearance. They are Gram-negative bacteria and are characterized by motile structures known as flagella.

Standard Candle: A standard candle is an astronomical object that has a known absolute magnitude.

Stegocephalian: A group containing all four-limbed vertebrates.

Stem Group: The classification of fossils that would not otherwise obey systematics based on living organisms.

Stereom: A calcium carbonate material that makes up the internal skeletons found in all echinoderms, both living and fossilized forms.

Sternum: A long, flat bone that protects the underlying muscles, organs, and important arteries within the chest.

Stipitate: Having or borne on a stipe (a stalk or stem).

Subduction: Where the oceanic lithosphere of a tectonic plate converges with the less dense lithosphere of a second plate, the heavier plate dives beneath the second plate and sinks into the mantle.

Sub-trapezoidal: A trapezoid with rounded corners.

Suspensory: Holding and supporting an organ or part.

Swim Bladder: An internal gas-filled organ that contributes to the ability of many bony fish (but not cartilaginous fish) to control their buoyancy.

Synapse: A junction between two nerve cells, consisting of a minute gap across which impulses pass by diffusion of a neurotransmitter.

Synapsid: One of the two major groups of animals that evolved from basal amniotes, the other being the *sauropsids*, the group that includes reptiles (lizards and snakes) as well as *crocodilians* and *dinosaurs* (birds).

Synonymisation: The identification of two taxonomic terms as synonyms, thus equating two potentially disparate categories.

Talon: Hooked claw.

Taxon: A taxonomic group of any rank, such as a species, family, or class.

Tectonic Plates: A massive, irregularly shaped slab of solid rock generally composed of both continental and oceanic lithosphere.

Teleost: A fish of a large group that comprises all ray-finned fishes.

Telson: The last segment in the abdomen, or a terminal appendage to it, in crustaceans, *chelicerates*, and embryonic insects.

Tendonous: Consisting of tendons.

Theia: A hypothesized ancient planet in the early Solar System that, according to the giant-impact hypothesis, collided with the early Earth around 4.5 billion years ago, with some of the resulting ejected debris gathering to form the Moon.

Thermophile (Adj. Thermophylic)**:** A bacterium or other microorganism that grows best at higher than normal temperatures.

Theropod: A carnivorous dinosaur of a group whose members were typically bipedal and ranged from small and delicately built to very large.

Therapsid: A fossil reptile of a Permian and Triassic order, the members of which are related to the ancestors of mammals.

Tidal Force: The *differential force of gravity* which arises because the force exerted on one body by another is not constant across the diameter in that the side which is the nearest to the second body is subject to more gravitational force compared to the side farther away.

Tomia: (*Sing. Tomium*) are the cutting edges of the two mandibles. In most birds, these range from rounded to slightly sharp.

Traps: Flood basalts forming a step-like landscape. This step-like landscape is the origin of the name 'trap rock' after the Swedish word 'trappa' which means 'stair step.'

Trochanters: Any of a number of bony protuberances by which muscles are attached to the upper part of the thigh bone.

Unguals: (from Latin *unguis*, i.e. nail) A highly modified distal toe bone which ends in a hoof, claw, or nail.

Unicellular: An organism that consists of a single cell, meaning that all life processes, such as reproduction, feeding, digestion, and excretion occur in one cell.

Uniformitarianism: The assumption that the same natural laws and processes that operate in our present-day scientific observations have always operated in the universe in the past and apply everywhere in the universe.

Vascularize: To develop or extend blood vessels or other fluid-bearing vessels or ducts.

Vegetative: Relating to or denoting reproduction or propagation achieved by asexual means, either naturally or artificially.

Vermiform: Resembling or having the form of a worm.

Vestigial: Of organs or parts of the body, degenerate, rudimentary, or atrophied organs, having become functionless in the course of evolution.

Vibrissae: Long stiff whiskers growing around the mouth or elsewhere on the face of many mammals, used as organs of touch.

Vicariance: The geographical separation of a population, typically by a physical barrier such as a mountain range or river, resulting in a pair of closely related species.

Viluy Traps: The Viluy Large igneous province, which includes the Viluy traps. They cover most of the present day north-eastern margin of the Siberian Platform.

Xanthroperin: A yellow, crystalline solid that occurs mainly in the wings of butterflies and in the urine of mammals.

Zygapophyses: Any facets of vertebrae that articulate with each other.

Epilogue

My granddaughter relates the story of a conversation she recently had with a college friend on 'Evolution'. "Ah yes." said the friend, "That's all about our coming from monkeys, isn't it?" The conversation came to an abrupt end!

The fact is that the subject of 'Evolution' is one that is so broad a topic and covers so many different disciplines, one interlocking with another.

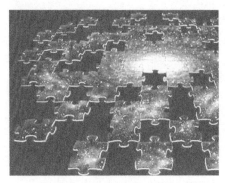

It is also often difficult to appreciate evolution's real extent and how one aspect is, at the same time, autonomous and dependent of others.

It is hard to accept that the Universe emerged from the singularity of a point of infinite density and gravity

... but what caused the Big Bang?

Quantum mechanics attempts to explain the beginning of the Universe through a series of quantum fluctuations which cause the Universe to expand and contract. Another theory predicts a universe being created after the old one is destroyed, each with different universal constants. Yet another theory relies on the fact that the Universe is perhaps one of many in a multi-verse, (*Stephen Hawking's 'no boundary' model ultimately posits that our universe is just one of infinitely many parallel universes.*) and has budded off from another universe as a result of quantum fluctuations, as opposed to our Universe being all that exists.

But interestingly, it has now been reported that a group of three researchers, associate professor at KEK Jun Nishimura, associate professor at Shizuoka University Asato Tsuchiya, and project researcher at Osaka University Sang-Woo Kim, have succeeded in generating a model of the Universe's birth based on superstring theory.

Using a supercomputer, they found that at the moment of the Big Bang, the Universe had 10 dimensions – 9 spatial and 1 temporal – but only 3 of these spatial dimensions expanded.

"Similar to imagining our Universe (or any three-dimensional space) being enclosed by a two-dimensional boundary, our three-dimensional space may in fact be the boundary around a higher-dimensional space." Bryan Brandenburg

One notable feature of string theory and M-theory is that these theories require **extra dimensions** of space-time for their mathematical consistency. In string theory, space-time is *ten-dimensional* (nine spatial dimensions, and one time dimension), while in M-theory it is *eleven-dimensional* (ten spatial dimensions, and one time dimension).

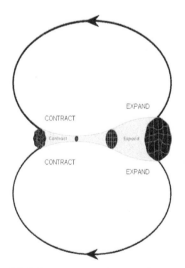

Given all of this, it is not outside the realms of imagination to consider the Universe as being either a **sphere** or a **torus**, because both are curved and closed. The curved/closed model is generally assumed to be a hypersphere, which has a surface volume of $2\pi^2 r^3$. Interestingly enough, the surface volume of a torus is also $2\pi^2 r^3$, so the spatial geometry of a curved/closed universe could just as easily be **toroidal**.

If this were to be so, it would answer the ever-begging question of 'what happened before the Big Bang'!

Now let us look at some of the figures that pertain to our Universe in general:

The deepest image ever taken, the **Hubble eXtreme Deep Field**, revealed 5,500 galaxies over an area that took up just 1/32,000,000[th] of the sky. But today, scientists estimate that there are more than ten times as many galaxies that Hubble, even at its limits, is capable of seeing. All told, there are some ~2 trillion galaxies within the **observable** Universe. However, the **James Webb Space Telescope** promises to significantly increase this number now that it has begun to send data back from its orbit one million miles away.

Carl Sagan once stated that *"there are more stars in our Universe than there are grains of sand on all the beaches on Earth"*. Such a statement not only leaves one to estimate the number of stars in the Universe but also a meaningful estimate of the number of grains of sand there are on Earth.

Firstly, the Milky Way galaxy has been estimated to contain between 100 and 400 billion stars. There are some ~2 trillion galaxies in the Universe with the high probability that this figure will increase significantly (*see above*). The lowest number of stars that can be found in the Universe based on the estimate of stars in the Milky Way galaxy is therefore between 2.0×10^{14} and 2.0×10^{16} stars.

Secondly, there is the question of the grains of sand … A single grain of sand found on the beach is half a millimetre in diameter. Twenty grains make up about a centimetre, and 8,000 make up one cubic centimetre. To calculate the volume of sand, you need to determine the amount of coastline that consists of sandy beaches. Dr. Jason Marshall *'The Math Dude'* estimates the volume of the beaches to be 700 trillion cubic meters. Mathematically, the figure amounts to 5×10^{21} grains of sand.

The mathematician suggests that this is just an estimate and the number could change by a factor of two to a low of 2.5 and a high of 10 sextillions.

A mathematical conclusion can be made that the least number of stars is equal to the highest number of sand grains. However, it is likely that there are five to ten times more stars than sand on the beaches. In 2016 researchers, observing images from the Hubble Space Telescope stated that there could be more than 2 trillion galaxies in the observable universe, which is ten times more than the highest number expected. This is in addition to the fact that the entire universe cannot be observed by any telescope on the earth.   *ref: Worldatlas.com*

But how large is the Universe?

The Sun is one astronomical unit (AU) away from us. One astronomical unit is 149,598,000km.

The Universe is 93 billion light-years across and is **expanding at the speed of light**. Just one light-year, is equivalent to 63,000 AU, or the equivalent to 9 trillion kilometres. So that works out as:

$$9.3 \times 10^{10} \cdot 6.3 \times 10^4 \cdot 1.49598 \times 10^8 \approx 8.8 \times 10^{23} \text{ km}$$
Light years   AU   km in one AU

or

8,800,000,000,000,000,000,000,000km   (or 8.8 septillion km)

That is how large our Universe is, and that is not even the end of it. The 93 billion years is just the **observable** Universe, the Universe which we can currently see. It has been suggested that the whole Universe might very well be 250 times larger than that which is observable by us.

Finally we must look at the number of possible universes, or multiverses, there may be in the greater firmament. That is not to suggest that all, of even a fair proportion of these universes are 'live' universes. They may be dead and totally void of any form of life, and then there are those which may be alive but dependent on entirely different astronomical and physical constants; their chemistry and bases for life may be quite different from those in our universe.

In a recent study, Stanford physicists Andrei Linde and Vitaly Vanchurin have calculated the number of all possible universes, coming up with an answer of $10^{10^{16}}$.

If that number sounds large, the scientists explain that it would have been even greater except for the fact that we, as observers, are limited in our ability to distinguish more universes. Otherwise, there could be as many as $10^{10^{10^7}}$ universes.

Somewhere within the Universe is the Solar System, insignificantly small when compared to the size of the Universe, but very significant insofar as it has appeared that life has been produced in a variety of forms on one of its planets – a singular event, or so it would seem.

The search for extraterrestrial intelligence (SETI) is a collective term for scientific searches for intelligent extraterrestrial life, for example, monitoring electromagnetic radiation for signs of transmissions from civilizations on other planets.

Scientific investigation began shortly after the advent of radio in the early 1900s, and focused international efforts have been ongoing since the 1980s.

The Ohio State SETI program gained fame on 15th August, 1977, when Jerry Ehman, a project volunteer, witnessed a startlingly strong signal received by the telescope. He quickly circled the indication on a printout and scribbled the exclamation 'Wow!' in the margin. Dubbed the *Wow! signal*, it is considered by some to be the best candidate for a radio signal from an artificial, extraterrestrial source ever discovered, but it has not been detected again in several additional searches.

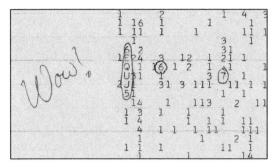

The Wow! Signal

Credit: The Ohio State University Radio Observatory and the North American Astro Physical Observatory (NAAPO).

In the meantime, however, a hint to the existence of extra terrestrial intelligence, albeit very slim, came in the form of a meteorite in 1969. In that year1969 a 100kg meteorite fell in Australia near the settlement of Murchison, Victoria. It belongs to a group of carbonaceous chondrites which are rich in organic compounds.

The age of this meteorite has been determined to be ~7 billion years old, about ~2.5 billion years older than the 4.54 billion year age of our Earth and the 4.6 billion year age of our Solar System.

Murchison samples contain common amino acids such as glycine, alanine, and glutamic acid as well as unusual ones such as isovaline and pseudoleucine. (A complex mixture of alkanes was also found to be similar to that found in the Miller–Urey experiment). Serine and threonine, usually considered to be earthly contaminants, were conspicuously absent in the samples.

The meteorite contained a mixture of left-handed and right-handed amino acids, where most amino acids used by living organisms on Earth are left-handed in chirality, and most sugars used are right-handed.

A 2010 study of one of the samples using **high resolution analytical tools including spectroscopy** identified no less than 14,000 molecular compounds, including ~70 amino acids.

The limited scope of the analysis by mass spectrometry though provided for a potential 50,000 or more unique molecular compositions, with an estimate of the possibility of millions of distinct organic compounds in this single meteorite.

So what implications has all this got to do with Evolution?

Firstly, considering the age of the Murchison meteorite, non-terrestrial life may well have begun at least ~7 billion years ago well beyond the realms of our Solar System.

Secondly, measured purine and pyrimidine compounds were found in the meteorite, and carbon isotope ratios for uracil and xanthine indicate, without a doubt, a **non-terrestrial origin** for these compounds.

Thirdly, that the vast number of molecular compounds and amino acids might even point to the basis of a system of life far more complex and advanced compared to anything witnessed on Earth throughout its 4.54 billion year history.

This meteorite demonstrates that many organic compounds may well have been delivered by early **extra terrestrial bodies** and might well have played a key role in life's origin and development.

Nor did the meteorite originate from either the Kuiper Belt or the Oort Cloud. The origin of the meteorite remains a complete mystery.

Kuiper Belt

Approximately 50 AU from the Sun, it is similar to the asteroid belt, but is far larger - 20 times as wide and 20-200 times as massive. Most short-period comets form their origins in the Kuiper Belt, and there are comets there with orbital periods of 200 years or less. In fact, it has been suggested that there could be more than a trillion comet nuclei in the main body of the Kuiper Belt. The largest **Kuiper Belt Objects** are Pluto, Eris, Haumea, Makemake, Quaoar, Sedna, Ceres, Ixion, Varda,

Gonggong and Orcus. These are often also referred to as Trans-Neptunian Objects (TNOs), Dwarf Planets.

Oort Cloud

The inner limits of the Oort Cloud begin at about 2,000 AU (0.032 ly) from the Sun. The cloud itself stretches out almost a quarter of the way to the nearest star, Proxima Centauri. It is spherically shaped and consists of an outer cloud and a torus inner cloud.

It is an extended shell of icy objects that exist in the outermost reaches of the Solar System and is thought to be the origin of most of the long-period comets that have been observed.

This cloud of particles is theorized to be the remains of the disc of material that formed the Sun and planets. The most likely theory is that the material now in the Oort Cloud probably formed closer to the young Sun in the earliest epochs of Solar System formation. As the planets grew, and in particular as Jupiter coalesced and migrated to its present position, its gravitational influence is thought to have scattered many icy objects out to their present position in the Oort Cloud.

Insofar as the cloud is very far away from the Sun, it can be easily disrupted by the nearby passage of a star, nebula, or by actions in the disk of the Milky Way. Those actions knock cometary nuclei out of their orbits, and send them on a headlong rush toward the Sun.

If we now come to the present day, we are faced with answering the transgressions of those who came before us and our present errors. The whole world is in crisis … the clock is slowing down. If nothing drastic happens in the very short time, we will be faced with the very stark reality of a Sixth Mass Extinction.

More than 500 species of land vertebrates have disappeared over the last 100 years. Many more animals will join those that have already gone. During the decade that has just ended (2010-2019), the International Union for the Conservation of Nature (IUCN) declared the extinction of **160 species**. Mankind has brought this about, and only mankind can make it right.

It is not only the extinction of species which is happening. No person on the face of this planet cannot help but notice the occurrence of global warming and the ensuing wide-scale destruction of forests and arable land. The rise in global temperature has been instrumental in floods throughout the world. As a gradual change in global warming, this may well have triggered mass migrations both on land and in the oceans and in turn initiating evolutionary changes.

Carbon emissions have not helped and, on top of this, it has been estimated that the world's oxygen will run out in a million years. But no one is doing anything really radical to address carbon emissions or depleting oxygen levels.

It is pure ignorant fallacy to insist that electric cars, for example, are the answer to the question of carbon omissions ... IT IS NOT!

"Electric cars may run on clean, green electricity, but purchasing millions of electric vehicles to replace our fossil-fuelled vehicles means overseas factories will pour out tonnes upon tonnes of greenhouse gas.

Although they produce just one-third the lifetime emissions of a petrol car, electric vehicles aren't completely clean. Carbon is created in the mining, manufacturing, shipping and recycling of the parts that make up every vehicle."

University of Toronto sustainable transport researcher Alexandre Milovanoff continues by saying: "The emissions from materials and manufacturing are a large chunk of a car's environmental impact".

From his calculations, a Tesla Model 3 emits the equivalent of 16.5 tonnes of carbon dioxide over a lifetime. That's about a third that of the Toyota RAV4, which produces 45.4 tonnes.

"The assembly of the Tesla's battery is the biggest contributor, contributing 6.5 tonnes of carbon dioxide. Furthermore, it takes a lot of energy to mine the lithium, nickel and cobalt metals required," he added "Then there's the battery creation. We need to add heat and electricity in order to change the form of those materials".

The vehicle body adds another 5.7 tonnes. Milovanoff estimates. "Conventional and electric vehicles will be mostly made of steel, cast iron and aluminium. ... Those are quite energy intensive to produce."

Because about 20 per cent of our electricity is generated from burning natural gas or coal, this will also add to an electric car's lifetime carbon footprint – about 4.3 tonnes for a distance of 200,000 kilometres. *Source: Olivia Wannan, 12ᵗʰ March, 2021*

But global warming, carbon emissions and oxygen levels have profound effects on population growth and vice versa.

Based on population growth, the economy doubled every 250,000 years from the Paleolithic until the Neolithic. Then the 'new agricultural' economy doubled every 900 years. Later on, dramatic changes in the rate of growth occurred more so as a consequence of technological advancement beginning with the Industrial Revolution in the 1750's than on any other single factor.

In his *'Essay on the Principle of Population'* which was published in 1798, Thomas Malthus predicted that whilst population grew in a geometrical progression and the supply of food grew through arithmetic progression there would come a time when there would be a drastic food shortage.

In the 'current era' the world's economic output now doubles every fifteen years, sixty times faster than during the 'agricultural era'. *"If the rise of superhuman intelligence causes a similar revolution,"* argues Robin Hanson of George Mason University, *"one would expect the economy to double at least quarterly and possibly on a weekly basis. This would place an intolerable burden to sustain the population".*

The current world population of 7.6 billion is expected to reach 8.6 billion in 2030, 9.8 billion in 2050 and 11.2 billion in 2100, according to a recent United Nations report.

With roughly 83 million people being added to the world's population every year, the upward trend in population size is expected to continue, **even assuming that fertility levels will continue to decline**.

Today, 'persons aged 65 or above' comprise the world's fastest growing of all age groups. Globally, for the first time in 2018, older persons outnumbered children under the age of five, and by 2050, older persons will outnumber adolescents and youth (ages 15 to 24). Some regions, such as Europe and Eastern Asia, already face a considerable challenge in supporting and caring for their older populations. As life expectancy continues to increase, older persons are likely to play more significant roles in societies and economies.

In fact the decline in fertility rates mean nearly every country could have shrinking populations by the end of the century, and 23 nations - including Spain and Japan - are expected to see their populations halve by 2100. Countries will also age dramatically, with as many people turning 80 as there are being born.

If the number falls below approximately 2.1, then the size of the population starts to fall. In 1950, women were having an average of 4.7 children in their lifetime.

Researchers at the **University of Washington's Institute for Health Metrics and Evaluation** showed the global fertility rate nearly halved to 2.4 in 2017 - and their study, published in the *Lancet*, projects it will fall below 1.7 by 2100.

As a result, the researchers expect the number of people on the planet to peak at 9.7 billion around 2064, before falling down to 8.8 billion by the end of the century.

Fertility rates are falling, but this has nothing to do with sperm counts or the usual things that come to mind when discussing fertility. Instead it is being driven by the greater emancipation of women with regard to education and work and acceptable societal norms. This has lead to women choosing to have fewer children.

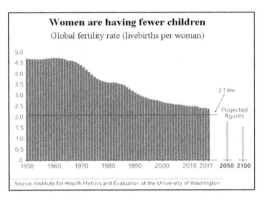

Women are having fewer children
Global fertility rate (livebirths per woman)

Source: Institute for Health Metrics and Evaluation at the University of Washington

Falling fertility rates can be regarded as a success story, but one that comes with a sting in the tail:

The study projects that the 'number of under-fives' will fall from 681 million in 2017 to 401 million in 2100 whilst the number of over 80-year-olds will increase dramatically from 141 million in 2017 to 866 million in 2100. In other words, demographically, there will be all the uniformly negative consequences of an *inverted age structure*,

The UK is predicted to peak at 75 million in 2063, and fall to 71 million by 2100. However, globally, 183 out of 195 countries will have a fertility rate below the replacement level.

The growth of human population impacts the Earth's ecological systems and thus evolution in many ways, including:

- **Extraction of resources from the environment.** The process of removing resources, in turn, often releases **pollutants and waste** that reduce **air** and **water quality**, and harm the **health** of humans and other species.
- **Burning of fossil fuels** for energy to generate electricity, and to power transportation and industrial processes.
- **Increase in freshwater use** for drinking, agriculture, recreation, and industrial processes

- **Forests and other habitats** are disturbed or destroyed to construct urban areas. As populations increase, more land is used for **agricultural activities** to grow crops and support livestock, leading to decrease of **species populations,** geographic **ranges, biodiversity,** and **interactions** among organisms.
- **Increasing fishing and hunting**, which reduces **species populations** of the exploited species.
- **Increasing the transport of invasive species**, either intentionally or by accident, as people travel and import and export supplies.
- **Transmission of diseases**. Humans living in densely populated areas can rapidly spread diseases within and among populations.

It is not surprising that humans created 'digital information'... perhaps it was inevitable. But now it has grown to such an extent that it has reached a similar magnitude to biological information in the biosphere. Since the 1980s, the quantity of digital information stored has doubled about every 2.5 years, reaching about 5 zettabytes in 2014 (5×10^{21} bytes).

In biological terms, there are 7.6 billion humans on the planet, each having, on an average, a genome of 6.2 billion nucleotides. Since one byte can encode four nucleotide pairs, the individual genomes of every human on the planet could be encoded by approximately 1.06×10^{19} bytes. The digital realm stored 500 times more information than this in 2014. The total amount of DNA contained in all of the cells on Earth is estimated to be about 5.3×10^{37} base pairs, equivalent to 1.325×10^{37} bytes of information.

> If all the strands of DNA in an average human were to be joined up nose to tail then the resulting strand would stretch to the Sun and back ~**610 times.**

If growth in digital storage continues at its current rate of 30 - 38% compound annual growth per year, it will rival the total information content contained in the entire DNA in all of the cells on Earth in about 110 years. This would represent a doubling of the amount of information stored in the biosphere across a total time period of just 150 years".

In the current stage of life's evolution, the carbon-based biosphere has already generated a human cognitive system capable of creating technology that will result in a comparable evolutionary transition.

It is argued that the human species currently dominates other species because the human brain has some distinctive capabilities that other animals lack. If AI surpasses humanity in general intelligence and becomes 'super-intelligent', then it could become difficult or impossible for humans to control.

Public figures such as Stephen Hawking, Bill Gates, and Elon Musk have expressed concern that full **artificial intelligence** could result in human extinction. Others believe that humans will evolve or directly modify their biology so as to achieve radically greater intelligence.

Digital technology has infiltrated the fabric of human society to a degree of indisputable and often life-sustaining dependence.

"Humans already embrace fusions of biology and technology. We spend most of our waking time communicating through digitally mediated channels... we trust artificial intelligence with our lives through antilock braking in cars and autopilots in planes... With one in three marriages in America beginning online, digital algorithms are also taking a role in human pair bonding and reproduction". Trends in Ecology & Evolution (2016).

Alexa and Siri have also had a not insignificant part to play (with the caveat that they should be turned off when sensitive or private conversations are being held!!)

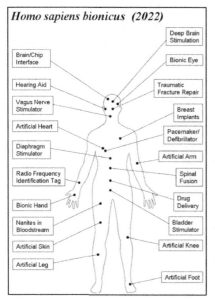

Homo sapiens bionicus (2022)

Deep Brain Stimulation

Brain/Chip Interface

Bionic Eye

Hearing Aid

Traumatic Fracture Repair

Vagus Nerve Stimulator

Breast Implants

Artificial Heart

Pacemaker/ Defibrillator

Diaphragm Stimulator

Artificial Arm

Radio Frequency Identification Tag

Spinal Fusion

Drug Delivery

Bionic Hand

Nanites in Bloodstream

Bladder Stimulator

Artificial Skin

Artificial Knee

Artificial Leg

Artificial Foot

Physical enhancements include cosmetics (plastic surgery and orthodontics), drug-induced (doping and performance-enhancing drugs), functional (prosthetics and powered exoskeletons), Medical (implants (e.g. pacemaker) and organ replacements (e.g. bionic lenses)).

Mental enhancements include nootropics, neuro-stimulation, and supplements that improve mental functions.

Computers, mobile phones, and Internet can also be used to enhance cognitive efficiency. Notable efforts in human augmentation are driven by the interconnected Internet devices, including wearable electronics (e.g. augmented reality glasses, smart watches, and smart textile), personal drones, on-body and in-body nanonetworks.

Many different forms of human enhancing technologies are either on the way or are currently being tested and trialed. A few of these emerging technologies include genetic engineering (gene therapy), neuro-technology (neural implants and brain-computer interfaces), cyberware, strategies for engineered negligible senescence, nanomedicine, and 3D bioprinting.

Mankind has readily adopted these physical and mental enhancements for a variety of different reasons, but what is more to the point is that the more humans become used to these enhancements so the more dependent they will come until a time will come when the panoply of enhancements becomes part and parcel of a new-day *Homo sapiens*.

As has already been stated, humans could well evolve, or directly modify their biology, so as to achieve radically greater intelligence. Many humans in the form which they are currently regarded will be a thing of the past having made way for a fully artificial intelligent being capable of total interface with technology - many, but not all! The fears of Hawking, Gates and Musk would be proved prophetic with the prescient warnings they had made of the future.

But this need not necessarily be the end of *H. sapiens,* or rather it **must not** be the end. Extinction is far too finite for a being such as *H. sapiens* to have journeyed for so long a time from the mud of primordial times.

The ancestors of *H. sapiens*, have demonstrated a remarkable tenacity for life notwithstanding the multitude of extinction events, severe climatic and atmospheric changes, and devastating effects of visiting comets and meteorites.

Surely *H. sapiens* is destined for something greater, more edifying than to mildly accept defeat, roll over and simply die an ignominious passing of an otherwise promising species. Yet it remains the only species throughout the history of life which insists on killing itself *en masse*.

H. sapiens has to 'grow up' and take responsible control of its destiny ... or it will most certainly go extinct and leave its artificial intelligence counterpart to rule the future.

According to a recent survey, the most precise estimates of species presently on Earth total some 8.7 million of which:

6.5 million species are to be found on Earth,
and 2.2 million species dwelling in the world's oceans.

These figures do not include micro-organisms and viruses. Of the 8.7 million estimate, only just over 953,000 have been described and catalogued.

Scientists have, moreover, estimated that over the course of Earth's history, anywhere between 1 and 4 billion species have existed on this planet.

It is rather humbling to realise that *H. sapiens* has been the only sentient being that has been raised to the high levels of consciousness that it now enjoys. It is true that many animals are sentient   (… and, in fact, lobsters even have legal status in British courts due to their high level of sentience. Moreover, New Zealand law bans *killing lobsters alive*, with Lacey Act in the USA also making it a federal crime with penalties ranging from $10,000 fines to 5 years in jail per violation). By 'sentience' is meant the faculty by which the external world is able to be perceived through the state of having sensory awareness or conscious sensations.

H. sapiens has gone that one step further in having a 'mind' of its own. By having a 'mind' is meant that humans have a set of faculties responsible for their mental phenomena. These faculties include thought, imagination, memory, will, and of course conscious sensations. They are functionally responsible for various phenomena like perception, pain, belief, desire, intention, and emotion. Ostensibly, it is the mind which raises *H. sapiens* to a level higher than all other species and is the subconscious but ever-present goad behind *Homo's* existence.

H. sapiens has had to travel a very long way along the evolutionary life-line from the closest unicellular living relatives to animals which date back to the *Choanoflagellates* some million odd years ago. Indubitably, a good deal has happened over the time spanning the creation of the first *Choanoflagellate* even to arrive at the putative example of the first primate in the form of the *Purgatorius,* which came to being just after the Cretaceous-Paleogene (K-Pg) extinction event some 66 million years ago.

Human Body

- Everything in this incredible, vast Universe is almost entirely, 99.9999999 percent empty space. If the space between the particles that make up all the atoms (and the spaces between atoms) were removed, i.e. compressed so that all the sub-atomic particles (electrons, protons, neutrons) were pressed together, **a human would fit into a cube 15 micrometres on each edge.** (15 micrometres = 0.015mm).

- The human body contains nearly 37.2 trillion cells. (3.72×10^{13})

- It is estimated that the microbial biome of our bodies, including bacteria and fungi, is around 39 trillion cells. (3.9×10^{13})

- An adult human body is made up of about 7 octillion atoms. (7.0×10^{27})

- The fastest muscles in a human body are the ones that make the eyes blink. They can contract in less than one-hundredth of a second.

- The average body makes about 2 to 3 million red blood cells every second, or about **173 to 259 billion** red blood cells per day.

- The body replaces around 330 billion (3.3×10^{11}) cells per day. At that rate, the body is making over 3.8 million new cells *every second*.

- The human eye can distinguish between approximately 10 million different colours.

- The human brain consists of 100 billion (1.0×10^{11}) nerve cells connected by 100 trillion (1.0×10^{14}) connections, more than the number of stars in the Milky Way galaxy. It uses as much energy as a 10-watt light bulb.

- The total length of the blood vessels in the whole body is **100,000 kilometres**, which can circle the Earth two and a half times.

- If all the neurons found in the human body are lined up together, they would cover a total distance of a 1,000 kilometres.

- The heart is a collection of individual cells, but it is the complex interaction of numerous cell types that give the heart its ability to pump blood. If heart cells were to be placed in a Petri dish some of the cells, called **myocytes**, will be seen to beat independently – and will continue to do so!

H. sapiens is, by any description, a highly sophisticated biological machine, as in fact are many present-day fauna, but in different ways and perhaps to a lesser degree. It is indeed barely credible that such a biological machine as *H. sapiens* is also a species which is sentient and mindful of its existence, perhaps as pure 'accidents' in the course of evolution.

It is true that, throughout evolutionary history, ancestors have had to survive the '*Ravages of Time*', to borrow the idiom from the Hong Kong comic series created by Chan Mou.

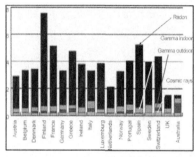

Average annual doses of radiation in different countries (in millisieverts per year). From Encyclopedia of Analytical Science (2005)

There have been extinction events, massive earth movements, volcanic eruptions, global warming, fluctuations in oxygen and ozone levels and greenhouse gas, not to mention background radiation. But perhaps, only perhaps, within the fundamental make-up of humankind, there is the ability to display a probabilistic nature of quantum mechanical phenomena just as particles were seen to do in Young's double-slit experiment in 1802 – everything is, after all, made of the same stuff! Could it be that not necessarily the paths of evolution, but the end scenario, is already pre-ordained for *H. sapiens*. Maybe mankind will develop other faculties; maybe it will be superseded by another more resilient species … and perhaps the class of *H. sapiens* which has readily adopted physical and mental enhancements will evolve into humanoid androids to leave the restrictive confines of Earth and explore the far reaches of the Universe. Pure science fiction? Maybe, but then again maybe not!

Recommended Further Reading

Anthropic Cosmological Principle	1988	Barrow, J D.
Cycles of Time	2011	Penrose, R
Dark Matter and the Dinosaurs	2017	Randall, L
Extinction: Bad Genes / Bad Luck?	1992	Raup, D M
Fossil Identifier	1994	Weidensaul, S
Grand Design	1982	Fay, S
Guide to Prehistoric Life	2005	Haines, T
Human Evolution	2009	Jones, S et al
Life: The First Four Billion Years	1999	Fortey, R
Natural History of Evolution	1993	Whitfield, P
Origin of Humankind	1994	Leakey, R
Origin of Species	2011	Darwin, C
Plundered Planet	2011	Collier, P
Sinking Arc (1980)	1980	Myers, N
Sixth Extinction (1995)	1995	Leakey, R et al
Voyage of the Beagle	1989	Darwin, C
Wonderful Life: (1989)	1989	Gould, S. J.

ed Readers Digest:
Last Two Million Years 1988 (en)
Merveilles et Mystéres de la Nature 1969 (fr)
Bildatlas der Tierwelt * 1971 (ge)

* Original in English:
  The Living World of Animals 1971 (en)

Mnemonic Devices for Geology

Order of geological time periods

Cambrian, Ordovician, Silurian, Devonian, Carboniferous, Permian, Triassic, Jurassic, Cretaceous, Palaeocene, Eocene, Oligocene, Miocene, Pliocene, Pleistocene, and Recent

> *Cows Often Sit, Down Carefully.*
> *Perhaps, Their Joints Creak?*
> *Persistent, Early Oiling Might*
> *Prevent Painful Rheumatism.*

Geological periods of the Paleozoic to Cenozoic

Precambrian, Cambrian, Ordovician, Silurian, Devonian, Carboniferous, Permian, Triassic, Jurassic, Cretaceous:

> *Pregnant Camels Ordinarily Sit Down Carefully,*
> *Perhaps Their Joints Creak*

Mohs' mineral hardness scale 1-10:

For **T**alc(=1) **G**ypsum(=2) **C**alcite(=3) **F**luorite(=4) **A**patite(=5) **O**rthoclase(=6) **Q**uartz(=7) **T**opaz(=8) **C**orundum(=9) **D**iamond (=10)

> *Tall Girls Can Fight And Other Queer Things Can Do!*

Order of sizes of rock matter
Boulder, Cobble, Pebble, Sand, Silt, Clay

> *Boys Can't Pass Social Studies Classes*

Order of crystallization of igneous minerals

Olivia's Parrots Actually Bite. So Pull Finger. Move Quick!

Olivine, Pyroxene, (Calcium Plagioclase), Amphibole, Biotite, Sodium Plagioclase, Potassium Feldspar, Muscovite, Quartz

- *The PC stands for Pyrox. and Cal. Plag.*
- *BS = Biotite and Sod. Feld – these minerals crystallize around the same temperature. BS and PC are a reminder that the order of crystallization is not as sequential as the Olivia-mnemonic suggests.*

International Paleozoic Timeline

Cambrian, Ordovician, Silurian, Devonian, Mississippian, Pennsylvanian, Permian

Can Oscar See Down My Pants Pocket?

Order of Geologic Era

Precambrian, Paleozoic, Mesozoic, Cenozoic

Pretty Polly Makes Cookies

Taxonomy Order

Domain, Kingdom, Phylum, Class, Order, Family, Genus, Species

Did King Phillip Cry Out "For Goodness Sakes!"?

Timeline of the Cenozoic Era

Paleocene, Eocene, Oligocene, Miocene, Pliocene, Pleistocene

Pigeon Egg Omelettes Make People Puke

First twenty elements, of the periodic table, with their atomic number

1. hydrogen H

2. helium He

3. lithium Li

4. beryllium Be

5. boron B

6. carbon C

7. nitrogen N

8. oxygen O

9. flourine F

Harry He Likes Beer Bottle Cold, Not Over Frothy.

10. neon Ne

11. sodium Na

12. magnesium Mg

13. aluminum Al

14. silicon Si

15. phosphorus P

16. sulphur S

17. chlorine Cl

18. argon Ar

19. potassium K

20. calcium Ca

*Nelly's Nanny Might, Although Silly Person,
She Climbs Around Kinky Caves.*

Printed in Great Britain
by Amazon

25769083R00188